I WILL COME BACK
FOR YOU

I WILL COME BACK FOR YOU

The undercover Jewish commando who helped defeat the Nazis

DANIEL HUHN
Translated by Rachel Stanyon

ITHAKA

First published in the UK by Ithaka Press
An imprint of Black & White Publishing Group
A Bonnier Books UK company

4th Floor, Victoria House,
Bloomsbury Square,
London, WC1B 4DA

Owned by Bonnier Books
Sveavägen 56, Stockholm, Sweden

Hardback – 978-1-80418-533-9
Trade Paperback – 978-1-80418-780-7
Ebook – 978-1-80418-781-4
Audio – 978-1-80418-782-1

A CIP catalogue of this book is available from the British Library.

Typeset by IDSUK (Data Connection) Ltd
Printed and bound by Clays Ltd, Elcograf S.p.A.

1 3 5 7 9 10 8 6 4 2

Every reasonable effort has been made to trace copyright holders of material
reproduced in this book, but if any have been inadvertently overlooked the
publishers would be glad to hear from them.

Rückeroberung was first published 2022 by Hoffmann & Campe, Hamburg
Based on the Audible Original Podcast *Befreiung* by Daniel Huhn, 2020

The quotation on page 151 is from Stefan Heym: *Nachruf*. Munich:
Bertelsmann 1988. The quotation is reproduced with the kind permission
of Mohrbooks (Zurich).

The translation of this book was supported by a grant from the Goethe-Institut.

Ithaka Press is an imprint of Bonnier Books UK
www.bonnierbooks.co.uk

For my father

CONTENTS

AUTHOR NOTE

The story described here is largely based on documents that the descendants of the Gans family granted me access to, especially five large boxes of letters and photos that are now stored at the United States Holocaust Memorial Museum (USHMM) as the Manfred Gans Collection. The most substantial part of this is over 1,000 pages of letters that Manfred and Anita sent to each other over ten years (between 1938 and 1948).

During the first phase of their correspondence (1938–1939), they wrote to each other in German. The extracts quoted here, and other sources quoted throughout for which there is no pre-existing English translation, have been translated into English by Rachel Stanyon.

The majority of the letters (those from 1943 to 1948) were written in English. These and other sources originally written in English have been quoted verbatim, including the original punctuation, typos and German–English sentence constructions (neither Manfred nor Anita were native speakers of English).

Hundreds of other letters that Manfred wrote to or received from his brothers, other family members and friends are also part of the Manfred Gans Collection.

Along with these letters, Manfred left behind several detailed travel reports, including those written after his journey to Theresienstadt in May 1945 and a later trip to Borken. He also wrote notes in day calendars from 1937 to 1943, which have also been preserved and offer insights in varying degrees of detail about his everyday life. Unless otherwise stated, all quotations in Chapters 1, 6 and 7 are from the report Manfred wrote upon returning from Theresienstadt on 20 May 1945.

The descriptions of Moritz and Else Gans's experiences are based mainly on correspondence with their siblings and Moritz's diaries, one of which he wrote during his time in the Netherlands and the other in the camps at Westerbork, Bergen-Belsen and Theresienstadt. Numerous other documents and files have provided further facts and clues to augment these comprehensive personal sources.

Many of the sources used for the research underpinning this book are accounts of events that were written down soon after they happened, and thus offer an immediate impression of the times. Where there are no contemporary records, I have been able to draw on a range of Manfred Gans's later reflections from interviews and his memoir *Life Gave Me a Chance*.

It is no longer possible to verify all the accounts, but extensive supplementary research in archives and books has confirmed what Manfred recounted in his letters and interviews. Inconsistencies between his versions of events and the official records are rare.

The descriptions contained in this book follow the sources, which are of such richness and quality that it is possible to closely trace this extraordinary life story. Very occasionally, and always with great caution, some scenes have been subtly augmented to provide atmosphere and some interpretations added by the author.

PROLOGUE

It is a windy summer's day in Goes, a small city in the south-west of the Netherlands. The market square is flanked by the soaring tower of the town hall and narrow redbrick houses, many of which have wooden planters filled with flowers by their doors. A flock of seagulls circles in the sky overhead; the coast is not far from here. The streets of this sedate city centre are deserted. The only thing disturbing the tranquillity of the morning is us: a cheerful tour group speaking in a jumble of different languages as it moves down the narrow streets, which feel like a film set built just for us.

In a car park at the edge of the city centre, a bus is already waiting, its motor running and doors open. Andy, our tour guide, is standing at the entrance, urging us to hurry: the road in front of us is long and there's a lot to do on the way. The last few suitcases are quickly stowed in the luggage compartment, and then Andy does a head count. We're all here. The door closes with a loud hiss. The bus is carrying 18 visitors from the USA and Israel. They are all descendants of the Gans family, from Borken in Münsterland, and are now travelling together for the first time to retrace their family history. At the back, in the last row of the bus, I take a seat, clutching my small video camera.

The bus begins to move. It's time to go.

I have the Borken municipal archivist Norbert Fasse to thank for my seat on that bus. He had called me just a few weeks before the trip and told me that, at the end of the month, he was expecting the descendants of a Jewish family that had once been well known in the town. He asked me whether I would like to do a few interviews with them. At the time, it was still unclear to both of us what might emerge from these conversations; at that point, I hadn't even heard of Manfred, Theo and Karl, or of Moritz and Else Gans – but something about their story made my ears prick up, and I readily agreed. Only later would I realise the true scale of their story.

When I embarked on this journey in 2016, I only knew where it would take me physically; I had no idea of the conversations and encounters that lay in store. For more than 1,000 kilometres, we followed in the footsteps of Manfred Gans, who had travelled through the ruins of his homeland in May 1945, searching for his parents: from the Netherlands, he crossed Germany to the former ghetto of Theresienstadt (Terezín) in modern-day Czechia.

I had only met the family for the first time the day before our departure, and, at the start, we approached our conversations carefully. I had a million and one questions, but I felt tentative, not knowing quite what I could or should ask. The days on the road were long, and there was often no time to conduct the interviews until we reached our hotel each evening – sometimes not until 11 o'clock. Nevertheless, we started trusting each other more and more, and the outlines of an impressive story grew clearer with every conversation.

After joining this journey, I visited some of the family in the USA and Israel and collected even more material on their family history. As I spent longer combing through the letters, photo albums and diaries, the complex story unfolding around Manfred Gans, his parents and brothers only grew more exciting. Out of my research and interviews, a newspaper article took shape, then a radio show and documentary film about the journey, and, later, a six-part podcast. Now, there is this book, too, which provides enough space to tell even more of Manfred Gans's turbulent and moving life story.

Following in Manfred's footsteps, this book touches on many major issues of its time: the fate of German refugees in England, D-Day and the remainder of the war, conditions in the Theresienstadt ghetto, discussions about Palestine as a place of refuge and Germany's broken post-war society. Insofar as possible, all this and much more is portrayed through the eyes and words of Manfred Gans, this book's main character, who not only lived through but also reflected on what was happening. To help put his world into context, short digressions offer explanations of places and events in the story.

Manfred Gans's life story offers a remarkable perspective on a time that remains difficult to comprehend to this very day: a time that, despite being shaped by an ideologically driven inhumanity, still shows evidence of profound humanity and that, even as it continues to recede into the distance, seems astonishingly current – especially in these days of social and political upheaval.

CHAPTER ONE

BACK TO THE BEGINNING

It is a sunny Saturday in Goes on 12 May 1945. By early after-noon, the thermometer has already reached nearly 30°C. A British officer, Frederick Gray, is packing a few things together: two street maps, a handgun, some rations and a letter from his superiors granting him permission to make his own way eastwards, which he had only received that day. The compassionate-leave slip written by the commander of 41 (Royal Marine) Commando states that 'all assistance should be given him to facilitate his journey'. He could certainly use some support. He plans to travel across the ruins of the German Reich, where the situation is chaotic and unpredictable. His goal is the Theresienstadt ghetto, near Prague, where he is desperately hoping to find his parents still alive.

Not long before departing from his base in Goes, a letter had reached Frederick Gray with news of his parents' whereabouts. It was from a relative, Erna, whom he hadn't heard from in years. She had learned that his parents, Moritz and Else, had still been in the Theresienstadt ghetto shortly before the end of the war. At this point, Frederick Gray hasn't seen them for five years and hasn't heard from them in nearly as long.

Just before they set off, Bob, Frederick's driver, discovers that the brakes on their jeep aren't working properly. Gray doesn't want to lose any time: at least 1,000 kilometres lie ahead of them, along with countless unknown challenges – every day counts if he wants to find his parents alive. Gray promises that they will see to the brakes along the way.

On 20 May 1945, just after his return, Frederick will write down his experiences of the trip: the pages, closely inscribed on a typewriter, are still held at the United States Holocaust Memorial Museum in Washington. In a concise and rather unsentimental style, like minutes, he writes:

> At last we are ready to push off. The driver has only been told about the trip quarter of an hour ago. He is all for it. Some people remark 'Lucky chap.' [. . .] The weather is perfect. We travel in shirt sleeves. [. . .] Leave GOES (South Beveland) round about 12 o'clock.

Fifty kilometres down the road, in Roosendaal, the two British soldiers pick up two Canadians who are returning from Brussels where they had been celebrating VE Day – the day of victory in Europe – just four days earlier. In London, hundreds of thousands gathered in Trafalgar Square; in Paris, people waved the Tricolour and danced in the streets; in Times Square in New York, confetti rained down. After six years of bitter fighting, peace finally reigns in Europe.

'Have we had a time!' the two Canadians proclaim. Now they must return to their unit in Bremen, and Frederick and his driver decide to take them to Münster, where they plan to rest that evening. But not long after, in Tilburg, they must stop again: the brakes are still playing up. They find a workshop, but the mechanic takes his own sweet time and Frederick starts to lose his patience. He decides on the spot that they should go on with the defective jeep. It is already late in the afternoon when they reach the banks of the Rhine River, which is running high in the spring of 1945.

The Rhine was the last major hurdle in the Allied troops' advance from the west, and, in the final days of the war, the Germans had blown up the remaining bridges over the river north of Bonn. Now, Bob must carefully manoeuvre the British military jeep across a makeshift pontoon bridge to bring them safely to the other side of the Rhine.

Having crossed the river, Frederick Gray is approaching familiar territory. Even though he is in a hurry, he decides to make a small detour.

CLEVE – EMMERICH – BOCHOLT, everywhere complete destruction. 'Bob' the driver who hasn't seen all this before just can't grasp it. The Canadians are cracking jokes, 'There is a house still intact over there, bloody natives living in it; far too good for them.' My maps are very small scale [. . .] still I know the country round here – the roads are appallingly bad. BOCHOLT is hardly recognisable. Total destruction. I think of the lovely days I spent here before 1938.

These 'lovely days' have long since passed. Back then, Frederick Gray didn't even exist yet, for our British officer grew up not in Great Britain but in the small Westphalian city of Borken. Manfred

Gans – as he was called back then – left his hometown seven years ago; now it is just fifteen minutes away.

When they reach Borken, Manfred asks his driver to slow down. He doesn't want to get out or even stop, but he does want to get an impression of the town. A rickety façade is all that remains of many of the houses; all that is left of others is a pile of rubble. From the school to the old post office, practically everything has been destroyed. The jeep turns in to Bocholter Straße. A few hundred metres later, Manfred finally sees his childhood home rising up proudly behind a huge tree. The high brick wall in front of the house has been demolished and a British flag is now flying from the flagpole in the front garden, but the house is still standing. The Allied Military Government (AMG) established its headquarters here just a few days before – it is one of the few houses in Borken still intact.

It looks very impressive. I am glad. That'll teach the Jerries. With their belief in mystic they will not fail to notice the lesson.

CHAPTER TWO

YOUTH IN BORKEN

Borken is in the west of the Münster region, not far from the Dutch border. Close to the Rhine, but out of the way of the larger cities in the area, the town is characterised by agriculture and the textile industry. In the 1920s, Borken had around 8,000 inhabitants, most of whom were strict Catholics. For more than 600 years, though, Jews had also lived in the town, and the Gans family was well respected there.

Manfred's grandfather, Carl Gans, had emigrated to Borken from the Netherlands. With the help of a matchmaker, he met Amalia Windmüller, the daughter of a long-established Borken family. Contrary to convention, which dictated that the bride move in with her husband's family, Carl followed his wife to Borken, where he established a textile wholesaling business. The couple had ten children: five boys and five girls. The fourth in line was Moritz, Manfred's father, a lively and ambitious child. At the age of 16, before finishing school, Moritz went to Frankfurt to learn his trade. Back in Borken, he and his four brothers eventually took over their father's successful company.

Moritz felt a strong connection to his hometown, but he had also learned to enjoy city life in Frankfurt. Every now and again, this drew him to Cologne to go dancing in one of the grand ballrooms, especially at Carnival. There, shortly before the First World War broke out, he met Else Fraenkel, an attractive, confident young woman, and the two quickly fell in love. But the war shattered their marriage plans. Like his four brothers, Moritz fought for the German Empire on the front, and he didn't return to Borken until after the war ended in 1918 – decorated with the Iron Cross, but also badly injured. Germany had lost the war; Moritz had lost a leg and a lung. But the engagement was still intact. A year after the end of the war, Moritz and Else married and settled in Borken. Moritz was already 33 by this time, and Else 27. They had waited for each other for six years. From that point, things happened quickly: within a short time, their sons Karl, Manfred and Theo were born. In between, they founded the company M. & E. Gans – En Gros Export. Despite challenging economic conditions after the First World War, the business flourished, and Moritz and Else eventually sold textiles and tailoring supplies throughout Europe.

In the middle of the 1920s, Moritz and Else bought a stately villa on Bocholter Straße, just a few hundred metres from the town centre. The entrance was framed by two columns, and a large balcony sat enthroned over a generous front garden. The Gans family employed housekeepers and gardeners, and, having only one leg, Moritz also hired a chauffeur. On weekdays, Moritz would go on business trips both within Germany and abroad, but he was always back in Borken for Sabbath – he had been brought up as an Orthodox Jew, and religious observance was important to him. The Gans household ate kosher and rested on the Sabbath. Else conformed to the Orthodox way of life out of love for her husband, although she herself came from a secular Jewish family.

*'The Pride of the German Fleet': Else Gans posing in the garden,
Borken 1931*

Else had grown up in Völksen, near Hanover. When she was young,
her parents sent her to a finishing school in Brussels. She was wild
about music and would write long, excited letters to her sisters
about the performance of a Wagner opera or the new recording of
a Mozart sonata. Else was sophisticated, modern and easy-going.
In the summer, she liked to walk through the garden in her bathing
suit, which was viewed critically both by her Catholic neighbours
and within the Jewish community. Unusually for the times, Else not
only appeared on the Gans company's letterhead, she was also a full
partner in the business. While her husband was travelling across
the country, she would be running the office, as well as raising the
children – with Prussian strictness, but a lot of warmth, too.

As well as being a successful businessman, Moritz Gans was very active in the community. He became the Borken district president of the Reich Association of War Disabled, and if a war-damaged ex-serviceman's pension was threatened with being cut, he would loyally step in. It was not uncommon for him to put his company staff to work on such matters, and his interventions were often successful. His efforts earned him respect among his fellow citizens, and Moritz was elected to the city council as a member for the Social Democratic Party of Germany (SPD) in 1929. He was Borken's first Jewish councillor, and one of only two representatives of the SPD at the time.

Even though (or perhaps precisely because) Moritz had himself spent four years fighting on the front, he became a staunch pacifist in the 1920s; politically, he had broken away from the militarism and nationalism of the German Empire long ago. While many people in Germany at the start of the 1920s were still reeling from the trauma of the First World War and the political upheavals of the young Republic, the Gans couple had a spirit of optimism about them.

There is barely a gap in Moritz Gans's appointment book of this time. Alongside his burgeoning business and political engagement, he was – of course – also active in the local Jewish community, eventually becoming the congregation's vice chairman. The community counted a good hundred members and had a synagogue and a small Jewish school. There, Manfred and his brothers learned arithmetic and writing, along with Hebrew, Jewish songs and the scriptures of the Torah. After the fourth grade, they moved to the Catholic academic high school. In the afternoons, though, they would continue to attend lessons with Bezabel Jehuda Locker, a Zionist-leaning teacher and polymath the community had brought specially to Borken from Poland. Education was highly valued in the Gans household, and the sense of family was at least as important.

Moritz and Manfred Gans in their garden in Borken, around 1938

Karl, Manfred and Theo grew up in a sheltered environment, surrounded by a large family. More than 20 family members lived in Borken and many more in nearby Holland. The bond and warmth of the extended family was especially apparent at Oma Amalie's birthdays, which fell on New Year's Eve. Year after year, everyone in the family – Amalie's 10 children and 19 grandchildren – would take a vacation and gather in Borken.

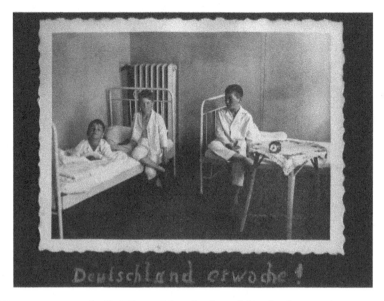

'Germany, awake!': Theo, Manfred and Karl after waking up, Borken 1931

Manfred and his brothers' everyday life is documented in a photo album from the time, which is dotted with little ironic comments: under the first photo in the album – in which you can see the three boys, still a little sleepy after waking up, but gazing curiously at the camera – is written 'Germany, awake!' This slogan was being stitched onto Sturmabteilung (SA, or Brownshirts) and Nazi banners at the time.

The boys have a bowl of porridge for breakfast, and then it's off to school. Karl is already proudly wearing his high-school cap, while Manfred and Theo go 'into battle' – as written in the picture's caption – wearing simple felt hats. At lunchtime, they eat on the spacious terrace, then scatter themselves across the roomy library to do their homework. Then they head off to play football at the Catholic-sponsored sports club.

For the time being, Manfred and his brothers still only occasionally experience instances of antisemitism. While it's true that they seldom go to the homes of non-Jewish friends, this is more to avoid accidentally compromising the Torah's dietary laws; most of their free time is spent outside on the streets anyway. In the evenings, the brothers read books or, preferably, listen to the radio. When it's time for bed, their well-polished shoes stand by the door, ready and waiting for the new day.

At the beginning of the 1930s, the Catholic town of Borken was still sceptical about the rising Nazi Party. During the Weimar Republic, the Catholic Centre Party always held a majority in the town, and it continued to do so even as the Nazi Party started gaining an upper hand in other regions. At face value, Borken's Jewish community, with its synagogue in the centre of town, was fully integrated; at least, the city's officials and church rarely missed an opportunity to highlight its happy coexistence with its Jewish citizens. But with Hitler's assumption of power in January 1933, the situation abruptly changed – and Borken was no exception.

Turning Point

It is a cold, damp day in Borken on 30 January 1933. Else is sitting at the table with her three children eating lunch; the radio is playing in the background. Suddenly, the newsreader interrupts the programme. The broadcaster announces that he has just received the following breaking news: President Hindenburg has appointed Adolf Hitler Chancellor of the Reich.

For the Gans family, as for millions of other people in the country, this news is not entirely surprising. Nevertheless, Else acts as if she has been turned to stone. The ten-year-old Manfred does not yet understand her sudden gloom. Over the following days at school, though, when he witnesses the joy that Hitler's appointment unleashes in some of his classmates, he realises that hard times lie ahead. He gets his first feel of this just a few weeks later.

On 1 April 1933 at 10 o'clock on the dot, after weeks of preparation, young men from the SA swarm across the country, positioning themselves and their campaign slogans in front of Jewish shops, offices and doctors' surgeries. 'GERMANS! DEFEND YOURSELVES! DO NOT BUY FROM JEWS' their signs read. Although shopping in Jewish stores is not (yet) forbidden, the Nazis are trying to use social pressure to disrupt the operation of Jewish businesses. The uniformed men admonish, berate and threaten customers who do not heed their call.

During both the German Empire and the Weimar Republic, the police and judiciary had often passively tolerated antisemitic agitators; now their actions were being decreed by the state.

Ever since Hitler had seized power, the press in Great Britain and the USA had been closely following and criticising the Nazi Party's actions. Soon after the takeover of power, Germany was threatened with trade boycotts. A furious Hitler blamed a conspiracy of international Jewry. His revenge was not long in coming: it found expression on 1 April 1933, the day known as the Anti-Jewish Boycott.

In Borken, the Brownshirts are positioned in front of a department store owned by the Heymans, a Jewish family. Manfred is at school.

Although it is a Saturday – the Sabbath day – and the three brothers are Orthodox, they are not excused from attending lessons; they can at least bring their books to school the day before so as not to have to carry anything, and their teachers allow them to refrain from writing. This Saturday, though, things are different. Just after 11 o'clock, Manfred's form teacher, Heinrich Tinnefeld, suddenly appears in the doorway and asks him and his three Jewish classmates to come into the corridor for a moment. Once there, he announces that they must leave the school immediately as he cannot guarantee their safety. Manfred, his brothers and the other Jewish students go home to meet their stunned parents. The news that Jewish students can no longer be kept safe in their own school makes Manfred's father furious. He uses his connections to extract a promise from the headmaster that, in future, he and other Jewish parents won't have to worry that their children will be harassed in class. Manfred, Karl and Theo go back to school again, but they are now considered outsiders once and for all. The three brothers and their six remaining Jewish schoolmates make a decision: from now on, they will keep the non-Jewish students at arm's length. They find this self-imposed isolation easier to bear than simply waiting for the other students to exclude them or for the school to mandate segregation.

A month later, on 1 May, the local branch of the Nazi Party holds a march in the city. Although Catholic groups in Borken were still suspicious of the National Socialists at the start of the year, they are now eager to join in the Nazi circus. On National Labour Day, the Catholic youth march in step with the Borken Hitler Youth.

Manfred watches the parade from the side of the road. Suddenly, in the middle of the crowd, he recognises a familiar face: his biology teacher, Peter Dahmen, whom he actually liked, is wearing the party badge now, too.

Everyday life at school under National Socialism changes steadily rather than suddenly. In German classes, disagreeable authors are struck from the curriculum. 'Physical education' is now on the timetable almost every day and is transformed into pre-military training for the older students. In history lessons, veneration of the heroes of Germany's past is hammered into the students, as are German claims to world leadership. Perhaps the most radical change is in biology, where 'race science' is moved to centre stage. In *Mein Kampf*, Hitler had proclaimed that 'No boy or girl should leave school without complete knowledge of the necessity and meaning of blood purity', and now his ideology is being put into practice.

In Borken, this responsibility is assumed by Mr Dahmen. In the race-science lessons he now oversees, he lectures on the physical and psychological advantages of the 'Nordic race' in comparison to other ethnic groups, especially Jews, as set out in the curriculum. Manfred's brother Karl is the first to be subjected to this instruction. Karl arrives in class carrying a two-volume edition of *Soziologie der Juden* by the Jewish sociologist and Zionist Arthur Ruppin. Mr Dahmen gives a lecture on why Jews are more often criminal and rarely socially engaged. For every one of the claims thrown into the room by his teacher, Karl has a counterargument. The students enjoy the spectacle, no doubt less out of solidarity with Karl and more out of amusement at this war of words between student and teacher, between David and Goliath.

Manfred in his school cap, Borken, around 1935

Two years later, race-science classes are on Manfred's timetable. When Mr Dahmen approaches the Jewish question again, trying to convince his students that the Jews are predisposed to being 'merchants', Manfred does the same as his brother. Once again, his classmates delight in the clash, but without taking Manfred's side. Manfred sums it up in his notebook: 'In the end, we don't trust each other at all anymore. The class has *rishes* – apart from the decent ones.' 'Rishes' is a Yiddish word for antisemitism.

Despite all this, a few members of the faculty are still trying to lend their support to the Jewish students, insofar as possible. When Manfred's cousin Karl-Heinz Gans passes his school-leaving examination in 1934, the last Jewish student to do so in Borken, the pastor and teacher Dr Engelbert Niebecker even ventures to make a point. In the oral Hebrew exam, he has Karl-Heinz translate a passage from the Old Testament ending with the following line: 'Vengeance is mine, I will repay, says the Lord.' The two uniformed Nazis on the examination board, presumably more ideologically convinced than biblically educated, fail to notice this sideswipe. Meanwhile, Karl-Heinz gets a 'very good' for the exam and, more than half a century later, still remembers this small victory.

Nevertheless, it is obvious that the Nazi regime's presence in the school is getting stronger with every month. Soon, swastika flags are flying in front of the building and portraits of Adolf Hitler hang in every classroom. As well as the German national anthem, school functions are now concluded with the Nazi Party's anthem. To avoid having to submit himself to this humiliation, Manfred usually sneaks out beforehand.

At the start of 1937, the headmaster, Dr Alex Hermandung, proudly announces that the flag of the Hitler Youth will be raised in front of the school building. Doing this is not just a matter of course, but a distinction for schools that can prove that more than 90 per cent of the student body has joined the Hitler Youth, a quota that the Gans boys' secondary school – the Borken Gymnasium – has recently reached. Compared with other schools, this is rather late.

By now, Manfred is one of just three Jewish students left at the Gymnasium. He finds the school day increasingly intolerable. One of the teachers no longer calls on Jewish students in class at all; another always gives them the worst marks out of principle.

Meanwhile, the local newspaper has long since been brought into line and now praises the abuses the Jews are subjected to as if they are good deeds. Only the press in the nearby Netherlands seems to find the developments concerning and regularly reports on the moral decline in its neighbouring country. One such article describes a Sabbath day in May 1935 when men from the SA pushed open the door to the synagogue in the Borken district of Gemen and, in the middle of the congregation's prayer, insulted, spat at and threw stones at them. Not long after this, the Nuremberg Laws ratified the extensive deprivation of Jews' rights. The last barriers had fallen. From that time on, anyone who continued to dare shop in a Jewish business risked being denounced a short time later in a *Stürmer-Kasten* – the name given to the glass boxes displaying the antisemitic propaganda newspaper *Der Stürmer*, one of which was in Borken's central marketplace.

With the increasing economic restrictions, Moritz and Else Gans have been forced to give up their offices in the centre of town, though they continue to operate their business from home as best they can. Not that long ago, they had been one of the most affluent families in Borken; now, the foundations of their economic existence have been stripped away. It is becoming increasingly clear that the only option is emigration.

Back in 1934, Moritz had established a company in Utrecht, Holland. He now starts using his office there along with his many business contacts abroad to help acquaintances leave Germany. He and his brother-in-law, Alexander Moch, have been following the situation closely and exploring various means of escape. In 1935, they travel to Palestine to get a first-hand impression of the Jewish settlements there and return with good news. Henny Schloss, Else's sister, emigrated there shortly after Hitler's assumption of power, and she and her husband have built a good life in Tel Aviv. She is prepared to receive one of the Gans children, but Moritz and Else continue to wait: the older the boys are, the easier it will be to let them go.

Just one year later, in 1936, the time has come. As the eldest, Manfred's big brother Karl is first in line. His father accompanies him all the way to Trieste, in Italy. A few days after his sixteenth birthday, Karl boards a ship bound for Palestine. While still aboard, he determines to shed his Jewish-Orthodox faith and his German name. He wants nothing more to do with either the country he was born in or the many religious conventions that have shaped his life until now, which Karl has long found narrow and onerous. He takes the name Gershon Kaddar and, while living in Tel Aviv, eventually graduates from the leading agricultural school, Mikveh Israel.

Gershon (still Karl to his family) finds out what happens next in Borken through letters from his younger brother, Manfred.

Despite all the restrictions and exclusions, Manfred is still managing to find variety in his everyday life, partly because his family still has some financial reserves. He explores the surrounding villages on his bicycle, builds elaborate model aeroplanes and even goes on short trips. He and his cousins visit Hamburg for a week and enjoy a full schedule of activities. He goes to the cinema regularly, rarely missing one of the booming film industry's box-office hits. He devours books by the German adventure and travel writer Karl May, but also eagerly reads novels and political literature by authors who have long been banned. Manfred plays music and takes photographs. Above all, though, he and a group of other Jewish youths meet up to have fierce debates on cultural and political topics. It all revolves around a few central questions: How long could they continue to stay in Germany? Where would they be able to find refuge and build a future? Manfred and his parents deliberate over various options: Should he follow Karl to Palestine soon? Or would it be better to prepare for emigration by going to one of the many recently established Jewish agricultural schools in Germany first? Then again, should he go to one of the Jewish boarding schools, which are supposed to be protected? Or would it be better to follow relatives and family friends to England or the USA?

While emigration plans are being hammered out hastily in the background, everyday life continues. In April 1938, Moritz Gans reads in the *Borkener Zeitung* that he must immediately register his remaining property with the tax authorities, who reserve the right to seize these assets 'in the interests of the German economy'. Moritz no longer finds any anti-Jewish measure surprising and has thankfully had enough foresight to take some of his money over the border in time. But Moritz and Else must soon close their business operations in Borken. From now on, they live on savings.

Even in these troubling times, there is one more big celebration. In May 1938, Moritz and Else invite a full household of people to celebrate the bar mitzvah of their youngest son, Theo. Long, stylishly laid coffee tables are stretched across three rooms with nearly thirty guests seated cheek by jowl. On the menu is fresh asparagus with tongue and salt beef, served with a 'modern salad'. This will be the last occasion to bring together the extended family – and the last bar mitzvah to be held in Borken.

By this point, even though almost everyone in town knows Manfred, Theo and their cousins, no one wants to be seen with or even talk to them anymore. The atmosphere is becoming increasingly hostile. One time, Manfred is shoved in the middle of the street. Another, he is beaten violently at boxing training because he is Jewish. In this context, the visit that summer from old friends of the Ganses – the Lamm family – must have come as a huge relief.

A Visit from Berlin

Leo Lamm and Moritz Gans completed their business education together in Frankfurt am Main and, even when Moritz went back to Borken and Leo established a company in Berlin, they stayed in close contact.

Like Moritz, Leo ran a textile wholesaler. With the elegant name Spitzen & Neuheiten (Lace & Novelties), it was situated prominently on Berlin's Friedrichstraße. Leo travelled from one fashion show to another throughout Europe, while his wife, Margarete (Gretel), was a trained pianist. Her world was the vibrant cultural scene of Berlin's Golden Twenties. Their daughters – Anita, who was one year younger than Manfred, and her older sister, Lilo – also relished Berlin life. Later, Lilo would remember how, when she and Anita went strolling along Kurfürstendamm at the start of the 1930s, every street corner would be abuzz with the widest variety of languages. The two sisters resolved to be at least as sophisticated as the people around them. But since they had not yet mastered any foreign languages, they invented a colourful mishmash of foreign-sounding, made-up words and exotic-seeming accents. Gesticulating wildly, they would drift past the cafés, cinemas and theatres, fervently hoping to be taken for well-travelled ladies from Russia, France or Italy. The two sisters were surrounded by this cosmopolitan spirit – until the Nazis corrupted this world, too.

Anita in Berlin, around 1937

Feeling the effects of the Nazi regime, the Lamm household – like the Ganses – had started making plans for emigration some time ago. For Leo and Gretel, the decision was clear: they wanted to go to the USA. But the United States was placing more and more limits on the influx of immigrants. Only those who could guarantee they would not be a burden on the American state could emigrate there: the Lamms needed an affidavit, a statement in which a resident of the USA guaranteed to take responsibility for their living expenses. They put all their hope in Herbert Piek, a cousin of

Anita's mother in New York who had a successful crockery and porcelain business, and therefore the necessary financial means for the much-coveted affidavit. A brisk exchange of letters between Berlin and New York began in 1937, and their entreaties were eventually successful. Herbert Piek vouched for the Lamm family at the American consul general in Berlin, opening the door for them to travel to the USA. Moritz Gans, in the meantime, used his contacts to organise passage on a ship for his friends.

The Lamms were some of the lucky ones. At around the same time as they were making their escape, a conference of delegates from 32 countries and 24 aid organisations was held at Évian-les-Bains on the shores of Lake Geneva to discuss the admission of Jewish refugees from Germany and Austria. The outcome was sobering. Apart from the Dominican Republic, no country was willing to accept a larger number of refugees. The USA put a cap on immigration from Germany and Austria: just under 30,000 refugees would be allowed to enter per year. Long lines formed in front of the consulates in Berlin and Vienna, and by the summer of 1938, the waiting time for a visa was several months.

At least for the Lamms, everything is now in place: their ship is due to set sail from the French port of Le Havre on 6 July 1938. With their suitcases packed, Anita and her parents – Lilo has gone on ahead – leave Berlin, stopping halfway at the Gans house.

When Manfred and Anita meet in Borken, it is a happy reunion. The two of them have already spent several summers together on a small farm near the village of Neuendorf, around 50 kilometres east of Berlin, where an educational institution for Jewish girls and boys was founded at the start of the 1930s.

Known as the Landwerk Neuendorf, it was one of the largest of many camps of the Hakhshara movement throughout the country at the time. Hakhshara's goal was to prepare Jewish boys and girls both vocationally and culturally for emigration to Palestine. Owing to the legal and social ostracism in Nazi Germany, Jews were also being deprived of career prospects. Jewish organisations reacted by creating vocational educational institutions, especially agricultural schools, which were intended to help pave the way to Palestine. Since January 1933, Landwerk Neuendorf had been headed by Alexander Moch, who, as well as being Manfred's uncle, is a friend of the Lamms. Neither Manfred and his brothers nor Anita and her sister received training there – they were still too young for that – but they regularly spent their summer holidays in Neuendorf, where they got to know each other better.

Just a few weeks before the Lamm family's visit, Manfred and Anita met up in Neuendorf, where they were surrounded by lots of other people their age. Now in Borken, they spend most of their time alone, roaming through the surrounding fields and woods. A photo from the time shows Manfred and Anita sitting on top of the family car. They are looking into the camera: laughing, light-hearted. Not long after, away from the camera up in the attic of the Gans house, Manfred and Anita kiss for the first time. They spend just four days together – long enough to fall hopelessly in love. But their happiness is short-lived. The Lamm family must keep moving: through Brussels and Paris to Le Havre, where they board the *Normandie*, the fastest, most elegant and luxurious ocean liner of its time. Their departure is full of mixed emotions – the pain of leaving is interlaced with the hope of living in safety.

On 11 July 1938, Anita and her parents are already gazing in wonder at the New York skyline on the horizon. Back in Borken, Manfred sits down and starts writing to Anita.

> What sort of people were on the ship? You sure must have had some fun! [. . .] Are you seeing and feeling lots of new things? It's a bit of a peculiar question, but I don't know how else to say it! I'm sure you'll know what I mean. Take in as much as you can yourself. This way, you mostly see things as they are; otherwise you're just looking through other people's eyes. I don't mean this for tourist attractions, just the things of utmost importance, like poor neighbourhoods, office buildings, etc. (12 July 1938)

Just a few days after the Lamm family's departure, Manfred starts preparing for his own journey. After Karl, he is next in line. His parents say it's only for the summer. He is to learn English in England, because in the autumn he will go to a Jewish boarding school near Berlin where he will need good knowledge of the language. Manfred is not disappointed at the news. On the contrary, he can hardly wait. In London – he hopes – he will be able to walk through the streets and talk to everyone again. It won't be forbidden just because he is Jewish.

CHAPTER THREE

ALIEN IN ENGLAND

On 13 July 1938, Manfred receives his visa for England and leaves Germany two days later. His parents take him over the border into the Netherlands. At the checkpoint, the family is thoroughly inspected. Moritz explains that they only want to visit relatives for Sabbath in Winterswijk, a small town just over the border. Unlike his parents, though, Manfred will not be returning to Borken. He stays for another night with his Uncle Bennie and Aunt Berta de Leeuw and then, on Sunday, takes the train from Winterswijk to Rotterdam. It happens to be the Jewish holy day Shivah Asar b'Tammuz, which would normally be a day of fasting for Manfred, who is conscientious about his religious practice; in the little pocket diary he carries on the journey, he confides that he 'half fasted'.

On the evening of 17 July 1938, Manfred boards a ship in the coastal town of Hoek van Holland that will take him to England. It is a departure for Manfred, but, even more, it is a new start.

A storm rages during the overnight crossing. Manfred is just 16 years old. He has studied hard at school to learn Hebrew, Latin and even French, but he barely knows a word of English.

In the run-up to his departure, Manfred's father used his contacts to arrange room and board for his son with a family in London when he first arrives. The Jakobs live in Golders Green, a predominantly Jewish neighbourhood in North London. Mr Jakobs is an insurance salesman and, appropriately for his profession, a sociable fellow. He spends many an evening with Manfred at the cinema or reading the newspaper. The Jakobs family is well connected in the Jewish community and introduces Manfred to a wide variety of people. Many of the relationships he forms in this time are lasting, and some will support him through his years in England.

Manfred now spends his mornings improving his English. In the afternoons, he goes on forays into the city. The boy from provincial Westphalia explores this English metropolis in amazement. At home in Borken, Manfred used to love wandering through the surrounding countryside alone. Now in London, he is one among eight million people.

Everything that he sees and feels during his first days in London, Manfred describes in his letters to Anita.

The people here are best observed in parks and shops. Have you also noticed that the common man here drinks an awful lot? It's almost as bad as in Borken. [. . .]

On Thursday, I went on my first bigger excursion. I travelled to Marble Arch and then went all the way across Hyde Park, but I found it really disappointing. After I'd got myself really lost, I stumbled upon Buckingham Palace and watched the guards in the barracks doing their drills there. Such nonsense!! [. . .] Then I marched back to Marble Arch, where a few people were speaking on soapboxes. One was arguing against the government; people made terrible fun of him. Then a Zionist spoke, calling for a Jewish state throughout Palestine. I could have nearly clobbered the chap to death. The people made terrible *rishes*. (2 August 1938)

Between 1938 and 1939, tens of thousands of Jewish immigrants arrive in England, including many children. Lots of families in England take in the young refugees, but part of the population is discontented and resistant. Manfred feels the tension and wonders whether people in England will become fascists, too.

Manfred considers following Anita to New York, but he'd rather not dip into his reserves to pay for the expensive passage just yet. And, Anita writes, antisemitism must also be feared in New York:

It could get dangerous, the Americans; I mean, the Jews here are like the Jews in Germany in 1925. Perhaps later, too. No one was aware of the danger then and no one is aware of it here. How much longer will it take for Hitler's ideas to spread all across America? They're already here to some extent. The Americans don't believe it: 'No, no, it can not happen here!' they say. I hope they're right. A huge wave of antisemitism is coming to New York through the immigration. It used to be surprising to meet a German here; now it's surprising to find an American on Broadway between 85th and 110th Street. (2 May 1939)

Anita is living in a typical 11-storey New York apartment block on the Upper West Side with her parents, fire escapes jutting out into the sky from the redbrick walls. She goes to school and is learning to sew leather gloves on the side. Her mother tramps between New York office towers selling nylon stockings. Her father, who sold textiles to top European designers before emigrating, is now working as a caretaker. Only her sister, Lilo, has found a good position, although it took a while. She is working at the German-language Jewish newspaper *Aufbau*, where she meets the co-founder and long-time publisher, Norbert Goldenberg, who later becomes her husband.

Not long after arriving in the USA, the Lamms start receiving requests for help from Berlin in large numbers. Acquaintances contact them asking for assistance with job placements or affidavits. Anita now spends her free time collecting donations for Jewish aid organisations on the streets of New York. Part of her is still caught up in Europe. She was unable to say goodbye to her friends in Berlin, and she has not yet found new ones in New York. Manfred remains her most important connection, a fact that Manfred is not entirely unhappy about: it means she still belongs entirely to him. He asks her to write to him as often as money allows, but adds:

> I don't think it's nice to become friends with someone only to then leave each other for years, and long-distance relationships are only for trashy novels. In real life, it's damned different. (9 September 1938)

Despite this, they continue holding on to parts of their old life, and Anita tells Manfred:

You write that you have a burning desire to know what will have become of me when we see each other again. So far, I can only tell you that I am still pretty much the same Anita, or at least that's how I seem to me. By the way, I don't wear make-up yet, despite having been here for seven months already. And I don't believe I have grown so superficial yet, either. I still have the same thoughts and ideas. I baulk at Americanisation; I'm really afraid of it, dreadfully so. (4 February 1939)

Manfred urges Anita not to cling to her old life too much. They will remain pen friends, he writes, but in these uncertain times, she shouldn't hope for more. Given the distance, he says, their young relationship does not have a bright future:

In general, something like this might last a year without seeing each other. Perhaps it will last longer for us because we're not among other people very much. But Anita, I don't want to make you sad. To be completely clear, this means: If you fall in love with someone else (and that is human, and only a sign of good health) then: be done with me! I wouldn't blame you for it one bit. I've already written you something similar. If we see each other again after a while and we are both still unattached, then very well, we'll start from the beginning again. If not, then each of us should find happiness in our own way. – Dear Anita, understand that I have written this for you and not to be beastly! When it comes to emotional matters, I can be a bit of a brute, but I couldn't be like that to you! Does that make sense to you? (27 October 1938)

A poem from 1939 called 'Emigrantensong', which Manfred likely came across during this time and which he kept his whole life, may shed some light on the extent to which Manfred, like Anita, is still finding his bearings in a foreign land. The poem is by Willy Katzenstein, a lawyer who came to London from Bielefeld in 1939. Katzenstein and Manfred didn't know each other, but what he wrote was very familiar to Manfred:

> Ich bin ein German refugee,
> There is no fatherland for me,
> Darum kam ich nach Surrey.
> Ich hab' still einen deutschen Pass
> And got my permit without fuss.
> Therefore darf ich nicht worry.
> [. . .]
> Bestimmt, life's difficult for us.
> At home, you see, da war man was,
> Hier ist man just a stranger.
> Man sitzt in Lyons' Corner House
> und pickt the other Germans raus,
> Freut sich, they're not in danger.
> [. . .]
> Ich träume of a Wunderland
> Where aliens are quite unbekannt.
> And also their restrictions.
> Ich wand're in a peaceful Welt,
> Wo Englisch wird phonetisch spelt,
> Und love is keine fiction.
> Doch on the whole bin ich content,
> I'm happy, dass mich keiner kennt,

Und fühl' mich like a gipsy.
Tomorrow ist's vielleicht vorbei –
What do I care, heut' bin ich frei,
Und Freiheit makes me tipsy!

Six weeks after leaving Germany, Manfred receives a letter from his father: 'What would you do if we asked you to stay in England?' His parents no longer think it is safe for him to return to Borken. Manfred is surprised by the news and at first doesn't know what he should do, as his residence permit is only valid for another few weeks. He draws up various plans only to reject them again. Then he contacts an acquaintance, Salomon Adler-Rudel, who, until his emigration, was the general secretary of the Reich Representation of German Jews in Berlin. Now in exile in London, Adler-Rudel administers several Jewish self-help organisations and has become an important adviser for many refugees. He counsels Manfred to sit the Matriculation Examinations ('Matric'), a school-leaving public exam that is a requirement for admission to some universities in Britain at the time, and then go to Palestine as soon as possible. Manfred is determined to follow his advice and enrols in a preparatory course at a tutorial college.

The ground under Manfred is constantly shifting, but he faces every new challenge as if it is not a burden but an opportunity. For as long as it holds, he seems to embrace every new decision wholeheartedly. This time, he writes to Anita:

Whether in war or peace, my place is only there [in Palestine] and that is true now more than ever. So, I will probably go to the Technion there. Under these circumstances, I doubt that I could still come to America in the foreseeable future. Anita, I hope you don't take the whole thing too hard: there is no point in it. I want to put all my personal sentiments aside in favour of the national sentiment, because that is the only thing that can satisfy me one hundred per cent. (22 August 1938)

Sometimes, Anita also dreams of building a new life in Palestine. Her best friend from Berlin has emigrated there, and perhaps Manfred would soon, too. He promises to fetch her as soon as he gets there.

Manfred's brother Karl and Anita's friend are not the only ones to have recently emigrated to Palestine. Sixty thousand Jews from across Europe had made their way there – partly because borders in the west were increasingly being shut. Just how difficult the situation already was for Jewish refugees by 1939 can be illustrated through the story of the MS *St. Louis*.

This Hamburg America Line transatlantic passenger ship left the port of Hamburg in May 1939, bound for Cuba. On board were more than 900 Jewish refugees, including Leo Haas from Borken, a close friend of the Gans family. But neither Cuba nor the USA would allow Captain Schröder to land. After days of negotiations, the *St. Louis* was finally forced to turn around. More than 200 of the passengers on board made a pact: if the ship really was sent back to Germany, they would commit mass suicide. But just before the *St. Louis* reached European waters, they received the good news that they could dock at Antwerp. The governments of Great Britain, France, Belgium and the Netherlands declared that they were each prepared to take in a small contingent of the Jewish refugees, although this itself unleashed renewed debate, as can be seen in the commentary on the decision in the London newspaper the *Daily Express* on 19 June 1939, which was not entirely sympathetic: 'The plight of these refugees wandering helplessly over the seas searching in search of a home, won the sympathy of the world. The decision to allow some of them to land in this country was approved by public opinion. This example must not set a precedent. There is no room for any more refugees in this country.'

Given the adversity facing Jews in Germany, the Jewish community in Palestine was urging the British government to raise the quota for Jewish immigrants there. Britain refused, citing concern that conflict with the Arabs could be exacerbated.

Before putting his plan to move to Palestine into motion, Manfred wants to have a qualification under his belt. He needs to pass his Matric in just four months, as there is neither enough time nor money for the regular eight-month preparation course. Mr and Mrs Jakobs try to point out the futility of his plan, but Manfred stakes everything on it. He studies from nine in the morning until midnight.

While Manfred is starting his preparatory course, Europe is on the brink of war. With strong rhetoric and a deliberate tactic of escalation, Hitler has been fuelling conflict with Czechoslovakia. He wants to annex the Sudetenland, bringing the ethnic-German part of the population in what was then Czechoslovakia 'back home to the Reich', and the Nazis have been making a concerted effort to unsettle the region. At the end of September 1938, the German Free Corps crosses the border to carry out raids on Czechoslovakian soil and to provoke a military reaction. Europe is holding its breath.

Manfred is following the political developments closely and writes down his thoughts almost every day in a long, episodic letter to Anita:

Saturday 24th
Everyone is talking rubbish about war. I don't believe in it! [. . .] Today they started handing out gas masks at all state schools, and people are lining up in front of them. Work is going on like crazy on every spare patch of land. At night, the sky is full of flak searchlights – practice drills. Civilians are reporting by the thousands to be Air Raid Wardens or join the Home Guard and the Territorial Army. People are starting to look for flats in the countryside.
[. . .]
Monday 26th, Rosh Hashanah
I listened to Hitler's speech from the Sportpalast! Now I believe there will be war, too! [. . .] What will happen to the German Jews when it gets going? Not a soul is going to bed. It might start as early as Wednesday!
[. . .]
Tuesday 27th
I'm getting myself a gas mask now, too. (9 October 1938)

In reality, it would take almost one more year for war to break out.

At the end of September 1938, leaders from Germany, Italy, France and Great Britain met in Munich to debate the 'Sudeten Question'. Without even involving the Czechoslovakian government in the discussion, the Munich Agreement promised the Sudetenland to the German Reich, and the impending war was warded off once more. Through this policy of appeasement, British

Prime Minister Neville Chamberlain and his French counterpart, Édouard Daladier, aimed to maintain peace in Europe. For a short time, the undertaking proved successful. But the appeasement strategy soon became a synonym for a weak and excessively passive British foreign policy.

Manfred is not impressed, either, adding to Anita that:

Wednesday 28th

[. . .] The Czechoslovakian question was the last chance for the democratic nations to stop Hitler. After all his threats of war, if I was interested in the existence of England and France, I would've made it clear to him that I wouldn't give him even an inch of Czech soil under *any* circumstances. With England, France, the USA and Russia against him in these 'war-threatening hours', Herr Hitler would not start a war! When all is said and done, he's not an idiot: he knows how to keep his head above water for a long time. England engaging in negotiations meant that victory was already on his side, and I just hope that England has not dug its own grave. But preparations for air raids are proceeding here at speed. (9 October 1938)

In these uncertain days, practically all Manfred's friends and acquaintances are volunteering for the Air Raid Precautions (ARP), the British emergency service responsible for providing protection against aerial attack. Thousands of people across the country are helping. Manfred ought to be helping, too, but he still hopes to get his German passport back and participation in the ARP could put him at a disadvantage at the German embassy. He is reluctant to take any risks while he has neither German nor British papers.

His background is now also becoming an issue with his schoolmates, as he tells Anita:

I laughed so hard last Thursday. It came out in school that I'm Jewish. I was talking to an Austrian, and he said to me, 'You'll be going back to Germany for sure.' I answered, 'Gee, how utterly naive are you? I can hardly go back as a Jewish refugee!' to which he replied, 'What? You're a Jew? We always thought you were the only German Aryan.' Now, just the day before, we had written an essay about badges and uniforms (English ones, of course!) and mine was read aloud. A moment later, five Germans came over to me, suddenly all so matey and completely different from usual. One said, 'When your essay was read out yesterday, I said that if they knew in Germany what kind of essays he was writing here, they would kick him out of the Hitler Youth!' When they found out that I was Orthodox, they were thunderstruck. (18 November 1938)

In Germany on the night of 9–10 November 1938, there were violent pogroms against the Jews, which became known as Kristall-nacht – the Night of Broken Glass. At around 10:30pm, a call came from Munich, where Hitler, Goebbels and other high-ranking Nazis were gathered, for all Nazi and SA offices in the country to start destroying Jewish property. Just before midnight, the head of the Borken Nazi Party, Hermann Upmann, received a call from the regional leadership in Münster that 'actions against the Jews' should start that very night. At the time, the Borken SA were having a drinking session at their regular pub. Meanwhile, out-of-town

SA men showed up and soon began smashing windows in Jewish homes. The riot organisers believed that, because these outsiders did not know the victims personally, they would be less inhibited. Nonetheless, as the night drew on, the SA men from Borken – some of whom were thoroughly drunk by this point – also joined in the attacks.

Back in London, Manfred reads about the destruction of Kristallnacht in the newspaper. A few days later, he receives news from home. His parents are fine. They were visiting relatives in Völksen during the riots and they are still there, unharmed. Manfred's younger brother, Theo, is staying with an aunt in Borken. He and a cousin had waited it out in the attic. They could hear the tumult in the street, but were not discovered. Twenty-nine Jewish men and women, including minors, were arrested in Borken on Kristallnacht. The Gans family house remains unscathed, but the town's Jewish institutions have been damaged.

Two days after the pogroms, Manfred's parents return to Borken. Moritz Gans heads out with his son Theo to inspect the condition of the synagogue. Although the interior furnishings have been destroyed, the building still seems to be structurally sound. Nevertheless, a short time later, Moritz is summoned by Mayor Grünberg, who announces that the Jewish community will either need to demolish the synagogue at their own expense or the town would have to be reimbursed 3,000 Reichsmark to pay for the demolition. Moritz responds that there are hardly any members of the Jewish community left in Borken, since almost all of them have either emigrated or been imprisoned, and that the community certainly does not have 3,000 Reichsmark at its disposal. On top of this, the building is still intact and doesn't need to be demolished. But the mayor stands his ground: the town is confiscating the property, there will be no compensation for the community and the synagogue will soon be torn down.

After Kristallnacht, the Nazis introduce a series of new measures that increasingly marginalise the remaining Jews in the country. They are no longer allowed to ride a bike or drive a car, own radios or typewriters, visit cinemas, swimming pools or restaurants, or set foot in forests or parks.

If it wasn't already, by now it must have been clear to Moritz that living as a Jew in this town has become impossible and, above all, unsafe. Moritz and Else take Theo straight to the Netherlands, from where he will travel to England with Alex Moch's daughter, his cousin Recha. Manfred is to meet them off the ship.

Manfred would miss their arrival if he took the first morning train from London, so he must leave the night before. Late in the evening of 3 January 1939 – it is cold and dark – Manfred goes to Liverpool Street Station. There are only a few people still about at this hour, and no young people at all, but Manfred has started enjoying these adventures more and more. He finds himself a seat on the Hook Continental, the same train that had brought him to London just a few months earlier. The heavy steam engine starts rolling towards the coast.

It is the middle of the night by the time the train reaches Harwich. The ship carrying Theo and Recha is not due until early morning, so he must now pull an all-nighter at the fishing port. All that penetrates the dark alleyways is snippets of conversation and a little light leaking from drinking holes. As a precaution, Manfred is carrying his small fixed-blade knife, but he still gets a fright when, suddenly, a man strides over to talk to him. To Manfred's relief, it isn't a crook, just someone from the Salvation Army who means him well. For a few pennies, he says, Manfred can sleep at the Salvos. After a short night, he heads for the ferry terminal at five in the morning. Despite the early hour, the wharf is abuzz with activity. Manfred watches anxiously as the ship approaches the harbour and docks. He is on the lookout for Theo and Recha. Then the time finally comes: from afar, he can already see the two of them walking down the gangway and, not long after, they are in each other's arms.

With the sun rising on 4 January 1939, they travel to London together. Manfred proudly shows them the big city, happy that he now has family nearby. Not long after their arrival, both Theo and Recha find accommodation at New Herrlingen (later known as Bunce Court School), a boarding school in the countryside that was moved from Herrlingen in Württemberg, Germany, to Otterden in the county of Kent at the start of the 1930s. It is now taking in Jewish children from Germany in large numbers.

In Great Britain, straight after Kristallnacht, a group of influential Jews petitioned Prime Minister Chamberlain to at least allow Jewish children from Germany and Austria to enter the country. They were successful. Over 10,000 Jewish refugees up to the age of 17 came to Great Britain through what is known as the Kindertransport. It was mostly Jewish aid organisations that organised the required guarantee of £50 per child (around three months' wages at the time) and accommodation: the British government wanted to prevent the refugees from imposing a financial burden on the country.

Once again, Manfred's uncle Alex Moch was involved in the efforts for Jewish youths. He had come from Brandenburg to England for the first time in 1938 and was now busy bringing as many schoolchildren as possible to safety to England. When on Kristallnacht the entire staff of his agricultural school, Landwerk

Neuendorf – where Manfred and Anita had spent several summers – was taken to the Sachsenhausen concentration camp and the young people there were threatened with a similar fate, he'd had to act quickly. Alex Moch went to England, negotiated with the German Jewish Aid Committee and finally found a suitable location to move the school to: the Tythrop Park manor house in Kingsey, Buckinghamshire. Manfred supported his uncle as an interpreter in these difficult negotiations. At the end of 1938, Alex Moch was able to both secure the staff's release from Sachsenhausen and bring more than 100 Jewish schoolchildren from the agricultural college to England. At Tythrop House, they could now continue their training from Neuendorf.

Manfred (centre) interpreting for Alex Moch on the left,
Kingsey, presumably 1939

In Manchester – Between Two Worlds

While helping his uncle organise accommodation and employment for hundreds of young refugees from Germany, Manfred must also find new lodgings himself. Room and board at the Jakobses' have become too expensive, and his attempts to negotiate the price are unsuccessful. So, he goes on the hunt and finds a cheaper room with a widow in the London Borough of Brent: among 'real people from the masses'. From there, he can still visit the synagogue in Golders Green and get to the tutorial college on the underground. Until recently, all Manfred had known was the solid middle-class environment of a rural town; now he is living in a working-class neighbourhood in a metropolis. He writes to Anita:

> I'm so free here at only 16 years old!! No one cares what I do or don't do, and no one tries to talk me out of my plans. Life here without friends makes you as hard as nails! [. . .]
>
> I know what you mean when you say you miss friends. I don't have any here either, but it's a bit different for me because I didn't have any real ones at home. But I won't be able to bear this situation for much longer, either. Grit your teeth and carry on regardless!! Just don't let on to the others that you are weak on the inside!! (December 1938?)

Mostly, it's not friends he misses so much as a sense of solidarity. He complains that even English Jews don't want to help any more. They all express their sympathy with the German Jews, but, on one occasion, when Manfred tries to secure lodgings for a young refugee, he is met with refusal. He even insinuates that the woman he is now living with, a Jew from Eastern Europe, has double standards: when she reads the newspaper, she vehemently bemoans all the injustices, but she won't let him keep studying after midnight as she doesn't want the electricity bills to cost too much. Somewhat cheekily, Manfred offers to pay a penny more each week to keep his lamp burning for longer: his exams are approaching.

Manfred studies and studies. In the end, though, it is not enough: he passes mathematics, mechanics and electrical engineering, but fails English. What vexes him most, he tells Anita, is his father saying, 'It's lucky that you've failed at something for once. You've had far too much luck up to now.'

With neither a school-leaving certificate nor prospects, Manfred goes in search of a job. He inquires at various organisations that help with job placements and is soon advised that he'd be better off trying his luck in Manchester. The chances of finding work in the industrial city in the north are significantly higher.

At this time, England is still feeling the impacts of the Great Depression and the high rates of unemployment that went with it – practically no one in London is looking for unskilled workers. So, Manfred takes the plunge and moves to Manchester. Once he arrives there, Manfred finds accommodation at Kershaw House, a hostel and meeting place for young Jewish refugees set up by the Manchester German Jewish Aid Committee. He writes to Anita:

Finally, good news! Out of the two million inhabitants here, there are only two hundred German Jews!! So there are good prospects. Hopefully our people will continue staunchly refusing to leave London. Then we got to the house. Thirty other boys and five girls live here. It's marvellous. Clean, good food, etc. People stay here until they have a job and an income. It doesn't cost a thing to stay here, and we even get two shillings pocket money. When they left us five newbies alone up in our room, we flung our arms around each other's necks in sheer joy. (27 January 1939)

But the search for a job in Manchester proves more difficult than expected. For the most part, factories require workers on Saturdays, which is unthinkable for Manfred as an Orthodox Jew. Eventually, he finds a position at the furniture factory J. O. Grant & Co. in Salford. He may have to work a lot of night shifts, but at least he has the Sabbath off. His employer – not a Jew but a devout Christian – is sympathetic towards Manfred's religious restrictions. He is put to work as a machine repair fitter, something which he, the son of a wealthy merchant, could hardly have imagined just a few months ago. But Manfred takes pleasure in the physical work and enjoys the proletarian atmosphere.

One day, one of the machines in the furniture factory conks out again, and Manfred and his co-workers must go in to repair it overnight. He and the machinist start taking the faulty unit apart. The thermometer in the dusty machine room reads 35°C. With their faces covered in a mix of sweat, dust and machine oil, they soon look like chimney sweeps.

There's one thing I certainly learned during the night, and that's how to swear. Under these conditions, you just can't get by without it. At 11, the machinist's wife brought us tea and cake, and at 3 a policeman showed up thinking we were soldiers from the Irish Republican Army. They are the folks making the regions around here unsafe at the moment. We came to talking about politics with him, and he asked me where I was from. When I said Germany, he said, 'Good thing I didn't come in cursing Hitler.' I just answered, 'I wouldn't have minded.' Then the machinist suggested throwing Hitler into the boiler. (8 May 1939)

Manfred's new acquaintances are not just from the working classes. One day, a guardian at Kershaw House presses an address into his hand and tells him he should go there that very evening. Manfred assumes he is getting the boot, since boys must move out soon after they have found work. Tired, disappointed and without knowing where it will take him, he boards a bus. When he gets off at the address given to him, he is standing before a splendid mansion.

A girl 'in uniform' opened the door with the message that 'the masters' were expecting me. Now I sure did feel damned uncomfortable, as I was still wearing my work clothes and hadn't washed (neither presentable nor kissable). For a moment, there was an internal battle between worker No. 252 from the company J. O. Grant and the formerly well-mannered son of well-to-do parents. This time, the latter was victorious, and I was determined to reveal a pure soul through my dirty clothing.

A man in a black suit and patent-leather shoes received me. He introduced me to his wife (both around 50 years old). Then they asked me if I had a job yet and what they could do for me. I was also to visit them frequently from now on. [. . .] All I could think was: 'You've got the wrong person. Someone mixed up the names at Kershaw House.' Then, finally, the woman revealed that the man I first lived with in London, who is still a close friend, had written that they should take me under their wing. (2 March 1939)

It was Mr Jakobs from London who had put Manfred in contact with the Steinarts, one of the most affluent families in Manchester. From this point on, they help Manfred, first of all by organising private lodgings for him. He is now also a regular guest at their house on Sabbath evenings. Over the coming months, Manfred continues to wander between two worlds: during the week, he is part of the Manchester working classes; on weekends, he keeps company with the gentry. On weekdays, he goes to boxing training; on the Sabbath, he discusses religious and political questions of Judaism with Rabbi Alexander Altmann, who had been a rabbi and professor in Berlin before fleeing Germany.

Meanwhile, his parents' situation in Borken has come to a head. In a devious perversion of the truth, the Nazis have blamed the Jews for Kristallnacht and are demanding compensation for the damage that they themselves caused. Across the entire country, houses and other possessions are now subject to forced expropriation, and Moritz and Else Gans's house in Borken is taken from them, so they must move in with Moritz's mother. Not long after, the Gestapo establish their headquarters for the administrative district of Borken in the Gans family home. The authorities will not pay any rent. The only thing Moritz can do is negotiate for them to receive passports to leave the country. The borders are still open, but every crossing is a gamble, subject to the whims of the official in charge. Since 1933, tens of thousands of political and Jewish refugees have already emigrated from Germany to the Netherlands – the largest immigration in the nation's recent history. The refugees are not always looked on kindly there; they are even met with animosity by many. In the eyes of many Dutch people, they are loud, arrogant and disruptive, though there are also some sympathetic citizens and mayors in the border regions advocating for German refugees.

For the time being, Moritz and Else remain in Borken. Else manages to go on a trip to England to visit Manfred. He is excited to have good cakes and biscuits from home, and takes his 'old woman' (as he called his mother) to a Zionist rally. Chaim Weizmann (who will become the first president of Israel), the British chief rabbi, Joseph Hertz, and representatives from the British government have been invited to discuss the question of Palestine. Manfred and his mother arrive too late: the hall is already completely overcrowded and has been cordoned off by the police. It is bitterly cold. The assembled crowd becomes more and more impatient, until finally they break through the police barricade. But the doors remain barred. Manfred grabs his mother and leads her to a side entrance. There he manages to convince a doorman to let him and his mother in.

And then I saw a political assembly that I will never forget as long as I live. That is, it was so bad!! Firstly, you don't

turn an excited crowd away from a political meeting
without at least one of the high-ranking leaders showing
himself to the masses or even talking to them briefly.
Secondly, the most senior leader of an organisation does
not take on the role of a doorman, as was the case with
Weizmann here, who kept announcing the individual
speakers. Thirdly, there should have been a Jewish guard.
(With fifty determined men, it would have taken me five
minutes to blow up the entire meeting.) (November 1938?)

Manfred does not agree with the substance of the meeting, either.
He thinks all they did was pussyfoot around. Only Rabbi Hertz
spoke well – he was the only one with the courage to criticise the
English government. Like large parts of the Jewish community
in England, Manfred is unhappy with the government's policies:
they are obstructing Jewish immigration in the British Mandate
for Palestine, and they are being much too timid in their confron-
tation with Hitler.

On the home front, Manfred's mother reports that his father
still has secret contacts and foreign currency, which he is using
to help smuggle refugees over the border into the Netherlands.
Manfred proudly tells Anita:

You could write books about how he is getting people
out, about how corruptible and drunken even the
German Gestapo is. One thousand guilders of foreign
currency can open any door. And Holland is also full
of opportunists who would do anything for money.
(2 March 1939)

A few weeks later, Manfred is sitting spellbound in front of the radio once more. It is the middle of March 1939. The Wehrmacht is moving into Prague and has occupied the rest of Czechoslovakia. After just six months, Hitler has broken the Munich Agreement. It is becoming more and more apparent that Germany wants war. Even British Prime Minister Neville Chamberlain has lost faith in the appeasement strategy. Manfred is now resolute in the face of impending war:

> In the event of war, I will use every means possible to try to go to Palestine. Do you think I'd shirk my duties? That's out of the question. If there's no other way, of course I'd fight on England's side first. I certainly don't have anything to lose, so why shouldn't one go in for the adventure? It seems to me that Hitler has pretty good prospects of winning, if he does it quickly. I know exactly what would happen next, but I'm not going to worry about it; I'll just see that I'm in Eretz by then. Then we can show it to those dogs again before they break us. (14 April 1939)

Manfred writes these lines in one of his last letters to Anita. After writing to his childhood friend nearly every week for around a year, he suddenly stops. In the letters themselves, there is no clue as to why the two of them cut contact so abruptly. All will be revealed later on: Anita's mother has intervened. She thinks Anita ought to be concentrating on her new life in the USA and forbids her daughter from continuing such an intense preoccupation with a boy who lives far away in England.

The End in Borken

In the summer of 1939, Manfred's parents are still in Borken. Their three children are already safely abroad. Hermann Finke, a trusted contact from the city administration, now warns them that they should leave the country urgently too. They set off immediately. At 8pm on 26 August 1939, Moritz and Else reach the border crossing at Kotten, not far from Borken. A small country road leads from here into the Netherlands. Heavily loaded with 11 suitcases and a few other bits and pieces, they stand before the customs officer. Moritz claims that they just want to go to the country for two weeks to meet their children. The customs officer is sceptical, but doesn't want to inspect the suitcases individually so soon before the change of shift. He gives the luggage a superficial examination and waves the pair through. They have got out just in the nick of time. Five days later, Germany invades Poland. By then, Moritz and Else are already in Zandvoort on the Dutch coast. They listen to the news of the outbreak of war on the radio. Two days later, the government in London declares war on Hitler. With this, Moritz and Else's visas for England, which they received months earlier, are now invalid. Else's mother manages to make it out of Germany, and then the borders are closed. For now, though, they are in safety and, despite war having broken out in Europe, Karl is even able to visit them from Palestine in September 1939. They brace themselves for a long wait while simultaneously planning their next steps. With emigration to England no longer possible, they set their sights on Kenya.

At the end of the 1930s, as the influx of Jewish refugees to Great Britain continued to grow, the British government started circulating plans to relocate some of them to the comparatively 'unpeopled' crown colonies. The politicians thought Kenya particularly suitable. The Germans were to be installed there as farm managers for the British land barons. A good 600 refugees eventually found their way to Kenya during this time. In early 1939, Else's sister Erna and brother-in-law Alex Moch also emigrated there, where they are now managing a large farm. But entry is expensive. When Moritz tries to collect the papers for Kenya from the embassy in Amsterdam, the consulate explains to him that the visa can only be issued if someone in Nairobi deposits a guarantee of 2,500 pounds – many times the annual income of a worker in England at the time. 'Father, I'm trying everything to get the guarantee,' Manfred writes to Moritz.

By now, Manfred has settled into life in Manchester. After his days working at the factory, he goes to evening school, and he passes his second attempt at the Matric in May 1940. But although he is earning enough money to support himself, Manfred's salary is not nearly enough to lodge the guarantee for his parents in Kenya. So, that escape route recedes into the background. Soon after Moritz and Else receive news that Manfred has succeeded in graduating, contact with their son breaks off.

On 9 May 1940, Moritz receives a telegram saying that their visas to travel abroad are finally ready for collection. His brother-in-law Justus Schloss in Tel Aviv has managed to arrange an entry permit for Palestine. Moritz plans to travel to the Hague right after Pentecost and get everything ready. But, once again, things do not go as planned.

In the early hours of 10 May 1940, the dull drone of German bomber wings can be heard throughout the Netherlands. Without officially declaring war, the German Wehrmacht invades its neighbour. Hitler's Western Campaign has begun. Moritz and Else spend the entire day sitting by the radio. Everything happens in a flash. The Dutch forces can barely put up any resistance to the well-equipped German army. At first, most people in the country still hope that Britain will rush to help them and chase the Germans out of the country. But this hope soon evaporates. It looks like the German troops will reach Zandvoort in just a few days. As a precaution, Moritz and Else pack their bags again. But it is too late; there is no longer any prospect of fleeing. On the contrary: the Dutch authorities intern all German men in the region.

Since the German ambush, the Netherlands has regarded Moritz as a member of an enemy nation. He is locked up in the disused garage of a barracks near Haarlem together with 300 other prisoners. But the inmates are treated well, and Moritz is not afraid of the Dutch like he is of the Germans, whose planes are now bombing the barracks. Given how quickly the Wehrmacht is advancing, the camp commander releases the German Jews from custody again a few days later, before the Germans can get hold of them. Moritz is free – but still in danger. In his diary, he writes:

> What now? – Should we try to reach England in a fishing boat? But what about mother? – We don't need to say much; we understand each other anyway. No, we don't want to make this likely futile attempt. The children are safe and we will soon see – we will master this destiny, too. (15 May 1940)

Moritz pays Jan Willem Smouter, an influential policeman in Zandvoort, 1,000 guilders to organise new passports for them:

ones that don't bear the 'J' that reveals their Jewish identity. They must lie low and be very careful, but with these passports they can live undetected in Zandvoort for a while longer and – even more importantly – they are confident that they have put enough water between Hitler and their sons. Exactly two years later, Moritz – who is now hiding on a farm – writes in his diary:

> When I was lying awake in bed this morning and thinking about our current situation, two thoughts occupied me. It is now three years since we had the last personal contact with our two youngest boys; two-and-a-half years since our eldest boy visited us in our involuntary refuge. The youngest had to leave us as a child; the two others as half-finished people. When the three of them were still in their parents' house under our guidance, we did everything by way of example to make them good, useful people, and gave them teachers and teachings that enabled them to face and master life, just as we have mastered it in the long years of our harmonious marriage, despite new worries every day. The fate forced on us Jews has separated us. Our only hope, which is what keeps us living here and fighting, is that one day we will be reunited with our three boys. (15 May 1942)

Enemy Alien

With Great Britain's declaration of war on the German Reich on 3 September 1939, all Germans in Great Britain were officially declared enemy aliens. Around 80,000 Germans in the country were summoned to specially established tribunals where they were interrogated about their attitude towards Hitler's regime. They were then classified into one of three categories: the few notorious Nazi sympathisers were assigned to Category A and imprisoned immediately; around 10 per cent were classified as Category B and monitored; and the vast majority received a Category C certificate and remained otherwise unaffected.

Manfred was classed as Category C. For now, he could continue to live his everyday life without restrictions. With the start of the Wehrmacht's Western Campaign in the spring of 1940, however, the situation changed. After the Netherlands, Luxembourg and Belgium, France was also forced to capitulate after just a few weeks, and the politicians in Great Britain were becoming increasingly nervous. They feared the British Isles would be invaded and imagined that the Germans living in Great Britain could be spies or saboteurs. Almost all Germans in Great Britain were summarily imprisoned, regardless of whether they were Category A, B or C, whether sympathisers or victims of the Nazis. Among them were around 60,000 Jewish refugees, including Manfred.

It is June 1940, and the time has come. A police officer stands at Manfred's door in Manchester. He questions him and then advises Manfred to quickly pack his belongings and store them somewhere safe. Manfred sells his treasured bicycle and has the rest of his belongings stowed away in the Steinart's cellar. A few days later, he is picked up by a police car and detained in an empty textile factory in Bury, near Manchester. The makeshift camp houses around 2,000 prisoners. In one and the same room, navy cadets loyal to Hitler and ultra-Orthodox Hasidic Jews receive their straw mattresses. The factory is dilapidated and the roof has holes in it. Luckily, the summer of 1940 is dry and mild. There is enough food, but, for devout Jews, it is now difficult to eat kosher. Manfred restricts his diet to vegetables and tinned fish.

After a few weeks, a high-ranking representative of the Jewish community in Great Britain comes to visit and asks the Jewish inmates for their understanding for their hasty imprisonment. He promises that they will soon be free. But it doesn't happen that quickly after all. From the crumbling textile factory, Manfred is next relocated to a makeshift tent camp in Prees Heath, north of Shrewsbury. Here, he is reunited with his cousin Hans-Fried Gans. The two of them grew up together in Borken, and Hans-Fried emigrated to England shortly before Manfred. Soon, Hans-Fried is allowed to leave the internment camp. He had become a Dutch citizen shortly before emigrating and is now being called up by the Dutch army in exile, for which he is released from detention.

Manfred, on the other hand, is shipped off to the Isle of Man, where the English have vacated and fenced off entire districts to detain more than 15,000 German, Austrian and Italian enemy aliens. The prisoners suspect they could be there for some time and begin to establish some structure in the camp. Orchestras and theatre troupes are formed; there are talks and workshops. Manfred, who is now 18, attends lectures in mathematics, mechanics and psychology, and dedicates himself to his study of the Torah – the camp certainly does not want for renowned rabbis. But not everyone can tolerate life in the camp. There is just one short entry in Manfred's diary for 1 November 1940: 'Suicide in House 9.' Then, three days later, the note 'Admission to P.C.' What had happened?

Under the new prime minister, Winston Churchill, Britain was increasing its war efforts. Churchill had committed the populace to 'blood, sweat and tears', and more soldiers were needed. Despite their status as enemy aliens, a few Jewish refugees had already been allowed to join the British armed forces voluntarily when the war started, although they had to be at least 21 years old to do so. With the danger of Germany landing in Great Britain mounting, this age was lowered. On 3 January 1941, Churchill said to Colonel Ian Jacob, 'I am very much in favour of recruiting friendly Germans and keeping them under strict discipline, instead of remaining useless in concentration camps, but we must be doubly careful we do not get any of the wrong breed.'

Churchill's position opened the army's door to German refugees. At the start of November, a British officer visited the young men in their camp on the Isle of Man and offered them the opportunity to join the army. This was a good – perhaps the only – chance to get out of the camp quickly. Manfred and the others complained that they would rather make the choice as free men, but, eventually, Manfred acquiesced. At the start of December, half a year after his internment in Manchester, he was set free. Just a few days later, on 13 December, he wrote in his diary: 'First day of drills.'

In the Pioneer Corps

The road out of prison leads Manfred to a base not far from Edinburgh in Scotland and the so-called Pioneer Corps, an auxiliary unit of the British Army that is neither armed nor designated for battle. Manfred slogs away shoulder to shoulder with convicted criminals and soldiers deemed 'not fit for combat'. He is frustrated, sure that he could do more.

Manfred's is a common story: in total, around 10,000 refugees from Germany and Austria served in the British Army during the Second World War; regardless of what training they brought with them, initially they were only allowed to help in the Pioneer Corps. They were assigned to build barracks, dig latrines or paint tanks – all extremely difficult tasks physically, but hardly demanding intellectually.

The only way Manfred is able to distinguish himself is through sporting competitions. He wins countless races and makes a name for himself in the army as a middle-distance runner. From now on, he regularly competes in sports competitions across the whole country. Apart from this, everyday life offers little diversion. When he has half a weekend day free, he takes the bus to Edinburgh with his comrades. Most of them spend their pay in the city's pubs. Manfred, on the other hand, buys himself a ticket to the opera.

On 22 June 1941, Manfred is just sitting down to breakfast with his unit when news starts circulating that Hitler has invaded Russia. Manfred quietly rejoices: he is convinced that Hitler has overreached himself and that the tide will soon turn. He hopes that Great Britain will now finally mount an offensive against Germany, and he is determined to be part of it. He applies to become a pilot in the Royal Air Force, but is rejected – it would be too risky to share information about aerial combat with an enemy alien.

The months that follow must have been stifling and isolating for Manfred. The Pioneer Corps offers little stimulation. Anita has stopped writing to him; his parents are in hiding; and even his day calendar is sparse. While war rages on the continent, Manfred, who from a young age has been intellectually and physically active, is in a period of stagnation.

Then, at the end of 1942, news reaches the young soldier that he should go to London for an interview. What the appointment will be about, he doesn't know, but this doesn't rattle Manfred: signs of self-doubt in his letters and journals are few and far between. He probably suspects that this meeting is an opportunity, perhaps the only opportunity he'll get. And he knows that he will grab it with both hands.

Chapter Four

A New Identity

On a cold January day in 1943, Manfred leaves his unit in Edinburgh and boards a train to London. A little snow had fallen in the night, but it has already melted in the hustle and bustle of the metropolis. Manfred stands in front of a huge redbrick building in north-west London – 222 Marylebone Road. For most of its history, this building has been one of the largest hotels in the city. In January 1943, though, those going in and out are mostly military brass.

Manfred enters the imposing building. It has more than 300 rooms. In one of them, right up in the attic, he is already expected. A rather inconspicuous but extremely fit young man in an officer's uniform starts off with a thorough interview. He asks about Manfred's previous occupations, his talents and goals. He also tests Manfred's mental state. Next to him sit two men in civilian clothing. They are from MI5, the British secret service, and subject Manfred to a lengthy interrogation. First, they want to make sure that Manfred is really Jewish. It isn't difficult for him to prove that and he names several rabbis in England who can vouch for his identity. Then they question him about his background, his parents and brothers, and want to know everything about their political views. Manfred has no difficulties answering these questions, either. Finally, at the end of the interview, a declaration is put in front of him: 'I hereby certify that I understand the risks to which I and my relatives may be exposed by my employment in the British Army outside the United Kingdom. Notwithstanding this, I certify that I am willing to be employed in any theatre of war.' Manfred signs. And then all he is told is to wait for further instructions.

Manfred still doesn't know what the meeting was actually about. He travels back to his unit in Scotland. It is over a week until he receives further news. Manfred is summoned to Bradford, a city in northern England. Once there, he learns that he should report to the train station in the middle of the night. There he meets 14 other young men. They are told what train to take and, without knowing where it will go, Manfred climbs aboard.

As dawn begins to break, the train pulls into Aberdovey, a tranquil coastal town in Wales. A group of young soldiers receives Manfred and his travel companions. They are wearing green berets – the distinguishing mark of the Commandos, a special forces unit in the British military initiated by Churchill. In Aberdovey, Manfred and the other newcomers are again met by the young man in the officer's uniform who had interrogated them in London. He is the unit's commander, real name Bryan Hilton-Jones, but everyone there calls him 'the Skipper'. It quickly becomes clear that the other commandos think very highly of him. Born in Wales, he is a determined, sporty type who speaks five languages. His German is perfect – practically accent-free.

Soon after their arrival, the newcomers are assembled in a manor house just outside the village. They each step forward to the Skipper in turn. He asks Manfred whether he has thought of a new name yet – he must give up his old one. Manfred is not prepared for this question and wracks his brain. Finally, it occurs to him: in the factory in Manchester, they always called him Freddy. The Skipper suggests that he keep the 'G' from his last name: 'Gray, that would certainly be a good name.' Just a few hours after his arrival, Manfred is handed a green beret and a new soldier's service book, which documents his new identity: Frederick Gray, Army Number 6387019. Special Services Brigade. Height: 5 ft. 10 ins., Weight: 158 lbs. Complexion: bright. Eyes: grey-green.

Manfred Gans as Private Frederick Gray, Aberdovey, 1943

Without ever having heard of it, Manfred has become a member of Three Troop, one of the most unusual and mysterious units in the British Army. After five years of oppression and marginalisation through the Nazis, and four years as enemy aliens, the young men now have the chance to make a significant contribution to the fight against Nazi Germany. 'In Aberdovey, we were reborn,' Manfred will remember in an interview many years later.

A year previously, Admiral Lord Louis Mountbatten, who at the time was Chief of Combined Operations Headquarters and himself of German descent, had planted an idea in the head of his friend, Prime Minister Winston Churchill. He suggested that some foreigners who had been forced to flee their homelands for Great Britain and now wanted to wage war against Hitler might be given the chance to fight with the British. Unlike some high-ranking military officers, Churchill found the idea convincing. In the early summer of 1942, the No. 10 (Inter-Allied) Commando was brought to life. Not long after, French, Dutch, Belgian, Polish and Yugoslavian troops were formed. And one more special troop would be created, under the greatest secrecy; even within the army, only a few were informed. Word has it that Churchill himself suggested calling it 'X Troop', after the mathematical symbol for the unknown. But X Troop sounded too suspicious to the military brass. Officially, the unit was thus to be called Three Troop: the third unit formed in the Inter-Allied Commando.

The members of Three Troop were all refugees, and almost all of them Jewish. They mainly came from Germany and Austria, with a few from modern-day Czechia, Hungary and Romania, and German was their mother tongue. Hilton-Jones had put out the search across the entire country for possible recruits for his unit.

Three-hundred and fifty candidates were interviewed in London and, from those, he selected around 90 to bring to Aberdovey. All who reported there were highly motivated and had a special aptitude. After the end of the war, Hilton-Jones would sum it up as follows, as quoted in Michael S. Goodman's account of Three Troop: they were distinguished by an utterly 'strange mixture of intense individualism and considerable troop spirit'.

Group photo of Three Troop, Aberdovey, 1943; Manfred is in the third row, fourth from the right

After they have received their new identities, Hilton-Jones makes it clear to the newcomers that their past lives are to remain secret at all costs. Even if they run into someone they know in Aberdovey, they are to deny their past; they must not react to their original names. It is also essential for the secrecy of the troop that they refrain from putting a single word about it to paper. The men are to destroy their personal documents: there could be no evidence of their former identity. No one is allowed to fraternise or correspond with people with foreign-sounding names, even with their own family. From now on, keeping a diary is also forbidden.

The high level of secrecy around Three Troop not only served to protect the individual soldiers, who would be subject to particularly harsh penalties if they were captured, it was also of utmost importance to the British military that the enemy did not under any circumstances learn of the existence of this German-speaking, elite unit in their ranks. How seriously the military leadership took the secrecy of the troop is made clear in an incident related by Peter Masters in his book *Striking Back*. Masters, an art student from Vienna, born Peter Arany, joined Three Troop not long before Manfred. A friend from Masters's previous unit who had not been chosen for Three Troop accompanied him to Aberdovey. Masters obviously thought nothing of bringing him along. Once there, however, it quickly became apparent that the uninvited guest presented a security risk. Straight after their arrival, the newcomer was arrested and carted off in a military vehicle. Masters accompanied him when he was put in front of the Skipper for questioning. In the presence of this interloper, the Skipper speculated with his sergeant as to how they could best get rid of him. Sergeant Major O'Neill suggested that he could accidentally fall out of a truck. The guest's shock was palpable. The Skipper strung him on for a little longer, before eventually reassuring him and letting the soldier go – but not without threatening that they would find him if he betrayed even the slightest thing about what he had seen or heard in Aberdovey.

Between the summers of 1942 and 1943, new recruits arrive in Aberdovey every few months. Manfred is part of Three Troop's second recruitment drive. At first, the new unit is viewed sceptically by the locals, but Captain Hilton-Jones encourages contact. Social evenings are organised, and friendships develop. Some of the soldiers and young women from Aberdovey grow close to each other, but the unit's background is always kept secret – even if the residents of Aberdovey must have puzzled over the not always entirely correct English and the often-conspicuous accents of the young 'British' soldiers.

On the evening of his arrival, Manfred is allocated a room in a private house. Since this unit doesn't officially exist, there is no barracks for Three Troop. Manfred is billeted with a single woman. When she asks her new lodger for his name, Manfred briefly falters. 'Call me Freddy,' he says curtly. He still needs to rehearse his new last name and his backstory. The Skipper had stressed that they needed to be armed for any situation. If someone were taken prisoner and interrogated, they had to know their fictional hometown as well as their real one. They must be able to describe where the local post office was, know the city's major textile manufacturers, what time the last tram left and where you could get the best bread. So that he wouldn't start fumbling if worst came to worst, Manfred mixes truth and fiction into a new biography. From now, anyone who asks about his past is told that his father was from England, but had spent years in Germany trading textiles, which is where he himself had grown up.

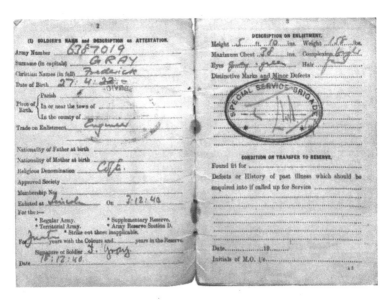

The soldier's service book of Manfred Gans alias Frederick Gray

With his new name and new life story, Manfred must set his Jewish identity aside. Almost every morning since his bar mitzvah when he was 13 – even during his time in the Pioneer Corps – Manfred has donned his tefillin, the Jewish prayer boxes. Even during his internment as an enemy alien, he ate kosher. But all this is now in the past. Under 'Religious Denomination' in his soldier's service book, it says 'C of E', shorthand for Church of England.

Despite, or perhaps precisely because of, its secret status, Three Troop has inspired many bizarre, heroic stories since the end of the war.

In 1982, James Leasor published his novel *The Unknown Warrior* about a Three Troop soldier who, in an audacious initiative as a British spy in occupied France, nearly turns the entire course of the war on its head. The book reads like a James Bond novel. Stephen Rigby, the protagonist, is not a real historical figure, or at least, none of the Three Troop commandos could remember a Stephen Rigby; the author evidently merged various biographies in his fictional character and had him enact some of the adventures that he learned of through Three Troop soldiers after the war. Manfred's archives also contain a long letter in which he describes his experiences to Leasor.

Then, in 2009, the film *Inglourious Basterds* picked up the story of a secret Jewish troop. In it, director Quentin Tarantino reinterprets the troop as a revenge unit. Lieutenant Aldo Raine, played by Brad Pitt, demands 100 German scalps from each of his soldiers. Manfred, like other veterans of Three Troop who learned of the film in their old age, was far from enthusiastic about it. They certainly had not reported for duty to kill as many Germans as possible, Wild West style. Their mission – both officially and personally – was to steal unnoticed into enemy outposts, procure useful information, come back alive and thus contribute to ending the war as quickly and with as few casualties as possible.

The training for Three Troop is extremely rigorous. What crops up the most in Manfred's calendar from this time is 'physical training'. The Skipper is a passionate mountaineer and believes that physical fitness is the main requirement for survival on the front. Physical training takes on almost the character of a religion. There are records of an exercise on Mount Snowdon, the highest mountain in Wales. For more than 80 kilometres, they march in full kit. Two soldiers are seriously injured while training in the mountains and subsequently decommissioned, but this is no deterrent – the drill continues. The elite soldiers climb and dive, learn how to parachute, steer boats and drive trains, and how to pick locks and make explosives. For a good year, Manfred and his comrades undergo what is perhaps the hardest and best training in the British Army.

Unknown Jo

In the autumn of 1943, Manfred is sent to Cambridge for a few weeks, where he receives additional secret-service training, including psychological interrogation strategies and details about the weapons and structures of the Wehrmacht. During this time, a letter reaches him from the USA, typed by a young American who calls herself Jo. Somewhat doubtful about the motivation behind her letter, he answers:

> Dear unknown Jo,
> it quite puzzles me why an American girl should want to write to a British soldier and I am very much inclined to think that – as you say – there is a catch to it.
> The continuation of this correspondence will depend on the following conditions:
> a) the next letter must be written in your own sweet handwriting so that with the help of some friends of mine who understand that business I may have your character analysed (highly unromantic I dare say but I am by nature suspicious)
> b) you must tell me how you got hold of that address under which you send letters to me if they are at all intended for me.

c) tell me all you know about me already, that includes
    the Regiment I serve in if you know it.

These conditions loyally fulfilled I have no objections to exchanging views and with an American girl.
(4 October 1943)

It doesn't take long for her reply to arrive. Jo is prepared to meet his conditions, and introduces herself: she is 20 years old and lives in New York. She goes to evening college and is supposed to become a teacher, but she has something else in mind. Her greatest desire is to join the US Navy Reserve for Women. She wants to help end the war in Europe more than anything, but her age and her family are standing in her way. This is why she wants to ask 'Freddie' all about his experiences in the military and what he was doing before the war.

The pair start writing to each other regularly, but – as Jo is soon to learn – must be constrained by Manfred's strict imperative for secrecy. One day, Jo receives a letter from a Luise Wislicki, whom she has never heard of before.

Dear Miss Garry,

I am the person who forwards your letters to Freddy [. . .] I am afraid, I had to cut out most of the questions you put to him in your last letter: - He is not allowed to say anything or even to hint where he is nor what he is doing. Events he can only report after three weeks have elapsed since they happened. We felt that if the Censor to the Forces got hold of your letter as it stood, Freddy might get into trouble. So I removed a few lines. Sorry. (1 October 1944)

Leo and Luise Wislicki are doctors from Berlin. After their escape from Germany, they ended up in Manchester, where Manfred met them through a mutual friend. The Wislickis, whom Manfred also lived with for a short time, are discreet people without children of their own – the perfect conditions for a cover address, which Manfred needs to send and receive mail without having to disclose his whereabouts or his new identity. When Manfred came to Three Troop, he named the Wislickis as his next of kin and listed their home as his address. Apart from them, only his brother Theo knows about 'Frederick Gray' and Three Troop.

Manfred continues corresponding with this unknown Jo from New York, but mostly reveals only general information about himself: he likes classical music and books, is 'mad on' sports and occasionally goes dancing. He either cannot or does not want to say more than this:

> The point is, that we hardly look at ourselves anymore as what we were before we joined the army [. . .] and in spite of the fact that we keep on looking forward to the day when we are going to be 'demobbed' the army has very much grown into us. (29 October 1943)

Manfred still seems to be somewhat sceptical about his pen pal. But after receiving a photo of her 'smashing beauty', he keeps up the correspondence; he must have suspected what becomes obvious in a later letter from Jo:

> As you know, a change of name is easy, does not mean too much and there are reasons for it.
>
> All this time I had been hoping that you would recognize me and must say that I have given you enough hints,

but for my name I have not hidden any truth and, as silly as it might sound, had hoped that you will remember an old friend in the US and was quite disappointed when you said that I was a 'stunning beauty' – which by the way is not true – but not 'that you know that face', at the time you received my picture. I hope you will not judge me too severely, although I am rather afraid of your verdict. [. . .]

Jeepers, Freddie, this letter is terribly hard to write, [. . .] it would be so much easier just to shake your hand and say: Shalom, remember? But since that is not possible, I hope my written handshake will do the job. [. . .]

I hope you are not too disappointed that 'Jo' and 'Anita' are the same person and you will be able to bear the shock and keep on writing to me. (1 February 1945)

So, the many letters that Manfred has received from New York are from his childhood friend Anita. Anita was unsure whether Manfred would write back to her at all, so she decided to get back in contact under a different name; and, because she still fears that her mother might forbid the correspondence, she has been using a friend's address for the exchange. Manfred is happy that the 'bluff' is now finally over and reassures her that she is quite wrong if she thinks that he wouldn't have answered her if she had used her real name. On the contrary.

Happy with this answer, Anita can finally speak openly, and she now wants to find out everything that she couldn't ask using her pseudonym.

Well Lt. tell me something about yourself, for inst. some things Anita would like to hear about, but which you could not tell Jo. How about your whole family, including the Mochs, do you ever hear from them? It is quite unbelievable how people who have been close to each other for years can drift apart so much. I have unfortunately heard of many cases of this sort and my thanks are great that I have been so fortunate to be together with my family. I hope Freddie, you too are one of those fortunate ones. (4 April 1945)

Manfred does not answer the question about his parents. Apart from the fact that he still needs to be careful with information about his identity, he doesn't know where they are. Until Germany invaded the Netherlands, he was still in regular contact with his parents. Since then, all that has reached him is occasional news by circuitous routes. The last sign of life his parents sent to England from their hiding place in the Netherlands is dated 1943, although it is unclear if this letter even reached Manfred at the time. In it, Else writes:

Yesterday morning, father was still lying down, but I could see in his face that he was thinking about something sweet. When I asked him afterwards, he said: I'm thinking of Manfred's 'boring life' [. . .] When this letter reaches you, it will be your birthdays, my boys, I would like to be able to deck your next birthday tables, then our wishes would have come true, then we could all play some nice records, hm? Stay in good health. You have us with you. (19 March 1943)

Earlier, in the summer of 1942, the German occupiers had evacuated large parts of the coastal town of Zandvoort to build bunkers for the so-called Atlantic Wall, a system of defences stretching from Norway to southern France designed to defend against Allied invasion from the sea. Moritz, Else and Else's mother, Bertha, were forced to leave the little house near the beach at Regentesseweg 11, where they had thought they would be safe. With the help of the policeman Jan Willem Smouter, they found a farmer in Marssum, near Leeuwarden, who would take them in. Shortly before going to ground, they gave Smouter and his life partner a box containing cash, securities and valuable jewellery. They asked the pair to keep their last remaining valuables safe for them and, if they should not return, to give them to their sons. Why and how Moritz and Else are later betrayed is unclear. In any case, around six months after they went into hiding, German Security Police are standing at their door in Marssum. Bertha is on another farm and manages to avoid being discovered, but Moritz and Else are arrested, taken to a prison in Leeuwarden and, a short time later, deported to the concentration camp Westerbork, where they are registered on 22 June 1943.

'Camp Westerbork' was built before the German invasion and had originally been designed to absorb the large number of refugees in the Netherlands, particularly Jews from Germany and Austria. In 1942, the SS seized Westerbork and transformed it into an assembly and transit camp. In July, the Nazis began rounding up all the Jews they could catch hold of in the Netherlands and sending them to Westerbork. Some of them had already spent time there after fleeing Germany, when it was still a place of refuge. This time, however, there was no hope of protection in Westerbork; instead, they were exposed to the tyranny of the SS. By the end of the war, more than 100,000 people would be deported from here. Every Tuesday, a train was sent east; almost all of them were bound for Auschwitz or Sobibor.

Once at Westerbork, Moritz and Else are separated into men's and women's barracks. Then, in the small hours of 14 September 1943, their names are read out on the list for the next transport. The train rolls into the camp early in the morning. Slave labourers have been made to lay a dedicated railway siding from the nearby station at Hooghalen to Westerbork to simplify the logistics of the deportation. The livestock wagons that are now rolling into the camp have neither seats nor windows. More and more people are loaded in. The SS guards check that all those whose names have been called disappear into the darkness of the wagons, while snarling dogs strain on their leashes. Then the engine starts to move.

At just after 7pm, the transport reaches the station at Soltau – a fateful railway switch point. The front wagons, loaded with over 1,000 people, travel on to Auschwitz, while the remaining seven wagons are decoupled, destined for the Theresienstadt ghetto. But the camp is overfilled and the engine is turned around. An hour later, the 283 occupants, among them Moritz and Else Gans, reach the platform of Bergen-Belsen.

At around the same time, Manfred and his unit are relocated to Littlehampton, a town on the English Channel. By the spring of 1944, the Allied forces have assembled in the hinterlands of the harbour towns in the area and the whole of southern England resembles one giant military training ground. More than a million US soldiers have arrived in England and at least as many British men are at the ready. Military and logistic preparations for landing on the European continent are in full swing, albeit amidst the utmost secrecy. Even Manfred and his Three Troop comrades don't know when and where it will kick off. The secret services on either side of the Channel begin a cat-and-mouse game: Who has what information? How much of it is true and how much is smoke and mirrors? 'In wartime, truth is so precious that she should always be attended by a bodyguard of lies,' Churchill is reported to have said to Stalin in November 1943, and great efforts are made to put the Germans off the scent.

Using the codename Operation Fortitude South, the Allies launch a large-scale deception manoeuvre. They marshal an entire phantom army: thousands of dummy tanks, aeroplanes and landing craft made of cardboard, wood and rubber are built and freighted to the coast to mislead German aerial reconnaissance into believing that the British Army is mobilising in the direction of Dover, from where it would cross to Pas-de-Calais. This would be a plausible strategy: the area around Calais is particularly suitable for a landing, offering the shortest passage from England; wide, flat beaches for the troops to land on; and the fastest route to the Rhine and thus to German soil. The subterfuge also involves airstrikes on radar and defensive installations, with targets in Pas-de-Calais attacked twice as much as those around the Allies' real landing site: Normandy.

The Three Troop soldiers are also being put to good use: individual members are ferried over to France on various special sorties, gathering information and laying false trails. In the spring of 1944, Manfred is chosen for a mission as part of Operation Crossbow. Together with three of his comrades, he is to be parachuted over northern France in the dead of night: one of them will have ropes; another a radio; someone will carry an infrared camera; and the fourth will have a cage full of homing pigeons. The target of their recce is a launching site for the V-1 flying bomb, which the Germans have brought into position in northern France and trained on England. The group's mission is to take photographs, send them back across the channel via the homing pigeons, and then beat their way to the coast, where they can rope down and wait to be collected by boats at night. Manfred and his comrades are already in the aeroplane when the campaign is suddenly abandoned – the wind is too strong. By the time the weather improves a few days later, the information has already been collected by another unit. Manfred is still yet to see any action.

Then, in May 1944, Three Troop is split up. Bryan Hilton-Jones had told the commander-in-chief the four areas in which 'his' soldiers would be particularly useful: firstly, questioning and identifying captured soldiers, because experience had shown that prisoners gave away more when they were interrogated in their mother tongue; secondly, guarding prisoners, since their knowledge of German meant they would pick up relevant information incidentally; thirdly, translating seized documents, which always had to be analysed quickly in case they contained valuable information; and lastly, during the commando units' reconnaissance patrols, where Three Troop's specialised training could be put to good use. To take advantage of their background and specialised training, Hilton-Jones and the military strategists agree that the Three Troop commandos would be most effective if spread across different units. So, for the entire duration of the war, this special unit never operate together. This is another reason why it has been hard to understand the significance of this troop as the story of a unit; instead, it has usually been viewed as a series of individual experiences.

Manfred is assigned to No. 41 (Royal Marine) Commando with three of his Three Troop comrades, Maurice Latimer (real name Moritz Levi), Tommy Swinton (Tamas Schwitzer) and Oscar O'Neill (Oskar Hentschel). The unit has a total of 450 men. On the evening of 5 June 1944, they board an invasion craft in Warsash, near Southampton. When darkness falls, they put out to sea. Slowly and silently, they head for France. After passing the Isle of Wight, they join the ranks of a convoy of hundreds of other boats. Around 80 soldiers are sitting tight in the hull of each open-topped vessel. Bottles of brandy are passed around to help brave the cold and wet conditions; Manfred favours a warm cocoa. Many aboard become sick on the open sea. The ocean is very rough that night: just the day before, a storm had passed over the south of England and, for a brief moment, Operation Overlord hung in the balance. But it has taken years to devise the plans for this day, and now there is no going back. A lot – perhaps everything – depends on how fast the Allies can gain a foothold in France, so that they can build a secure bridgehead on Continental Europe, ensure a line of supply and thus advance into the interior. A successful landing could mark the beginning of the end of the war in Europe. Failure would make every subsequent invasion incomparably harder.

Luck is on the Allies' side. In the early hours of the morning on 6 June 1944, the sea starts to calm and, with first light, they are met with an impressive sight. Black shapes start emerging along the entire horizon. As they grow bigger, they turn into aeroplanes. There are thousands of them in the sky overhead and just as many boats on the water. It is D-Day, and well over 100,000 Allied soldiers are on their way to one of the Second World War's largest military operations.

The combined forces of Great Britain, the USA and Canada are determined to drive back the German Wehrmacht on the European continent. Among them is Manfred Gans, although no one on the boat knows his real name. They are headed straight for the coast of France. The men take it in turns to look through the hatches of the invasion craft and report back to the others on what they see. Explosion after explosion lights up the coast. It takes another good hour to reach the Normandy beaches.

CHAPTER FIVE

RECAPTURE

At dawn on 6 June 1944, it looks like it will be an overcast day on the coast of Normandy. US troops are the first to reach shore at Omaha Beach, under heavy fire. Soon after, at around 7:30am, British units arrive at Sword Beach, the easternmost of the five landing sectors in the bay. Among them is the 41 Commando and Manfred Gans, alias Frederick Gray. The landing crafts get as close as possible to the beach and then lower their ramps. They are still a good 100 metres from the shore. With heavy packs and under constant fire, the commandos wade through knee-deep water. They are in luck: the resistance of the German troops is not as fierce here as it is a few kilometres further west, and they are able to reach the shore with considerably fewer casualties than the Americans.

The beach is ravaged, littered with the wounded and the dead. It offers no cover. Some of the Wehrmacht's *Widerstands-nester* (resistance nests) up in the dunes have already been destroyed by shelling from the fighter planes and battleships, and their machine-gun fire is slowly letting up, but grenades are still raining down from further inland. Manfred recalls the words of warning from General (later Field Marshal) Montgomery, the commander-in-chief of the British troops. Shortly before D-Day, he had visited Manfred's barracks and warned the soldiers that, on previous amphibious landings, British troops had tended to become 'beach happy': overjoyed at having solid ground beneath their feet, they would forget to leave the unprotected beach as quickly as possible. At the time, Manfred had determined never to make this fatal mistake. Now, he dashes across the beach and comes upon a group of just-captured German soldiers. While his comrades disarm and lead them away, he does a speedy interrogation and ascertains how to navigate the minefield. The information from the German soldiers turns out to be reliable, and Manfred manages to lead a few of his fellow commandos across the beach. They reach the designated rallying point in safety.

The 41 Commando has landed below the town of Lion-sur-Mer. The unit's first order of duty is to capture the town's German base and then fight their way 5 kilometres westwards to join forces with Canadian units in the neighbouring village of Luc-sur-Mer. Incessant explosions and gunfire heighten the morning's turmoil, and the entire coastal region is blanketed in the overbearing smell of explosives. As Manfred and his unit approach Luc-sur-Mer, they come under attack, and a well-hidden German anti-tank gun destroys all three of their escort vehicles. Luckily, a few Frenchmen open their doors, providing shelter to the British commandos. Their situation remains uncertain. With a small group of men, Manfred feels his way forwards from farm to farm. Unlike his comrades, who are in heavy army boots, he is wearing light shoes with rubber soles, making him quicker and – even more importantly – quieter. But they still don't reach Luc-sur-Mer until the

evening. Once there, they set up quarters in an abandoned farmhouse, but sleeping within solid walls seems too dangerous to
Manfred – mortar shells are still striking incessantly all around
them. He finds a hiding place between two low stone walls behind
the house, where he can eat something and rest for a few hours.
He is in dire need of this, for the following nights will be sleepless.

The Wehrmacht High Command had been expecting an Allied
invasion. What they didn't know was when and where it would
happen. In the spring of 1944, German occupied territory stretched
from Nordkapp, the northernmost point in Norway, to the Bay
of Biscay in the south of France. For three years, the Germans
had been busy building the Atlantic Wall, which was supposed to
protect what Hitler dubbed 'Fortress Europe' from Allied invasion. By D-Day, the Germans had built more than 10,000 defences
along the coast and buried over 6 million mines in the beaches – or
had them buried by prisoners of war and slave labour. Despite this,
Hitler and his generals must have realised that the approximately
3,000 kilometres of coastline could not be protected equally well
in every location, and German military strategists had been spec-
ulating about the precise location and exact time of the Allied
landing. They were not in agreement. The commander-in-chief
of the Wehrmacht in the west, Gerd von Rundstedt, assumed
the landing would be in Pas-de-Calais, at the narrowest point
on the English Channel. Field Marshal Erwin Rommel, who was
responsible for securing the Atlantic Wall, also suspected that the
invasion would begin in northern France, but he was not settled
on Pas-de-Calais and flagged Normandy as another possibility.
Hitler remained undecided. Sometimes he believed the invasion

would be in Norway; then he would move to Denmark; another time he would mention the Mediterranean. While Rommel would regularly inspect the defences and army units in France and von Rundstedt was living in Paris, Hitler himself never once set foot in the region. In the spring of 1944, he was spending most of his time enjoying the alpine panorama of his property in Berchtesgaden in the Bavarian Alps, where he had established his headquarters. From the mountains, he regularly contradicted his generals' military expertise – including when it came to the expected time of the invasion.

On the evening of 5 June 1944, reports from von Rundstedt that the radar stations on the coast kept being jammed had already reached Hitler's headquarters. At 1:30am, paratroopers were sighted east of Caen, a strategically important city in Normandy. But von Rundstedt's High Command in Paris only put a few units in Normandy on standby. Because wind, rain and heavy cloud cover were forecast for the coming days, hardly anyone thought that these individual reports of enemy movement would be the beginning of the invasion. That night, a few generals were at a military exercise in Rennes; others were having a good time in Paris. General Field Marshal Rommel – who had always stressed that the first 24 hours after the invasion would decide its success or failure – travelled back to Germany to celebrate his wife's fiftieth birthday.

In the early morning of 6 June, when news started pouring in about heavy bombing on the Normandy coast and boat sightings were reported, von Rundstedt wanted to move the 21st Panzer Division, the strongest group in the region with around 20,000 soldiers, towards the coast. For this, though, he needed Hitler's approval: the Panzer divisions were Hitler's favourite, and he had reserved the right to make decisions about their movement himself. But, because Hitler had a habit of getting up rather late and no one on his staff dared wake him, he only became aware of the scale of troop movement in Normandy late in the morning, after he'd had breakfast. Certain of victory, he said that the news couldn't be better. He believed he finally had the Allies where the Wehrmacht could beat them.

Nevertheless, without leadership or the coordination of information that would go with it, there was hardly any concerted counterattack until the afternoon. Too late, the 21st Panzer Division was ordered to the coast. Instead of driving the Allies back decisively, all they could do was temporarily halt their advance. On the evening of D-Day, Hitler, Rommel and von Rundstedt were still in agreement that the landing in Normandy was only a diversionary tactic for a later invasion from Pas-de-Calais. More than 150,000 Allied soldiers had by now already landed on the shores of Normandy and seized a 30-kilometre stretch of coastline, thus securing an important bridgehead for further supplies. But the bad weather prevented a rapid advance, and not all of D-Day's operational aims were achieved. The British had wanted to capture Caen on the first day of the invasion; the battle over the city would last another six weeks.

At first, Manfred and his unit barely made any ground after the landing, either. They had to hold out for longer than planned in the farmyard of a young Frenchwoman whose husband had been taken prisoner by the Germans. The Wehrmacht's initial counterstrike was easing off, and the Allies were occupied with establishing headquarters and building storehouses for the supplies. The coast was full of seemingly endless convoys of trucks and tanks rolling along the smallest of streets. Manfred and his comrades joked that you were in more danger of getting injured in a traffic accident than in battle in Normandy. But their impression of the situation was soon to change.

Patrols

After three days in Luc-sur-Mer, the 41 Commando moves out. Five kilometres to the south, near the village of Douvres-la-Délivrande, there is an important German radar station that the Allied troops have still not managed to capture after several attempts. A garrison of some 200 men is stationed in the two large bunker complexes, Hindenburg and Moltke, and, since D-Day, dozens of German soldiers who were unable to hold their position on the coast have also retreated to the heavily fortified facility. Although the base has not been able to stop the British from gaining ground in the area, the remaining units are still sending the Luftwaffe important information about the movements of the Allied troops. Its capture is thus of the utmost importance for the Allies' continued advance.

The radar station is protected by two tall barbed-wire fences, with a 300-metre-wide minefield between them. Over the following nights, Manfred goes on several reconnoitres to scope out the situation. These missions are initially only outside the complex, but then they are told to go in: they should cut through the barbed wire, cross the minefield and survey the two bunkers. Manfred is well prepared for such assignments and extremely driven, but he is not overconfident: he is, after all, still a realist. Before setting out, he writes a farewell letter and asks a comrade to give it to his brother in England if he doesn't return. Before the ink has even dried, he turns his full attention back to the mission.

After darkness falls, Manfred sets off with Maurice Latimer and Oscar O'Neill, along with three other soldiers. It takes them just under half an hour to cross the minefield. Manfred has come up with his own technique for this: he cautiously moves himself forwards in a squatting position while holding one hand out in front of him, carefully checking the ground with his fingers. This allows him to advance faster and, above all, react more quickly than if he were crawling on all fours as he was taught in his training.

Once they arrive at the fence around the bunker, they cut through the barbed wire and carefully approach the heavily fortified base. The massive armour-plated doors leading to the underground bunker are sealed. All the soldiers seem to be entrenched within the facility. Suddenly, a watchdog starts whining. Three Troop trained for situations such as this, but now they lack the right tools. They have neither the chemicals needed to poison the dog quickly and inconspicuously, nor a knife. Shooting the dog is out of the question – it would attract too much attention. 'Fighting, yes; suicide, no' is Manfred's matter-of-fact motto, and he and his companions quickly withdraw. The very next night, Manfred tries again with a new patrol. This time, they are forced to break off while crossing the minefield because one of them missteps and triggers an explosion. They manage to bring their badly injured comrade back before being seen. The commanding officer decides they have gathered enough information. The time has come. Several units of British soldiers and nearly fifty tanks attack from three sides. The men of the 41 Commando storm the northern part of the complex. The British force is vastly superior and the German soldiers, who have been holding out in the bunker for 11 days, are exhausted and afraid. The fighting only lasts a short time before a white flag is pushed through a slit in the door. In German, Manfred tells the enemies to surrender. The heavy steel door slowly opens and 150 soldiers emerge with their hands in the air. Manfred looks for the most senior officer so that together they can persuade the forces in the second bunker to surrender, too. When they arrive there, the other German soldiers are already emerging with their hands up. Not long after, the heavily fortified radar station has been taken and, with it, one of the Wehrmacht's last strongholds in the region has fallen.

Manfred gathers the prisoners, just under 300 of them, climbs onto a little hill and bellows at the crowd: 'Stramm gestanden, links um, Marsch vorwärts!' – commands he is familiar with from his school days in Borken. To his comrades' astonishment, Manfred's orders are followed at the double. Their march to the coast, from where the prisoners will be evacuated to England, takes three hours. Some of the newly arrived tank crews they pass on the way stop, look out of their hatches and ask jokingly whether there are any Germans left for them.

After the beachhead in Normandy has been secured, most of the Allied troops head for Paris. The 41 Commando, meanwhile, is to advance eastwards. So as not to make themselves an easy target for the Germans, they avoid the streets and carve their way across fields and through woods, mostly at night, often crawling along the ground. Little by little, they take the small villages along the coast.

In October 1942, Hitler issued what is known as the *Kommandobefehl*, a secret edict stipulating that all members of

Allied commando units were to be executed. This order – which contradicts the Geneva convention 'relative to the Treatment of Prisoners of War', by then already in force – was often followed, not least because to defy it was a punishable offence. In any case, it is clear to Manfred and the other Three Troop commandos that they could not, under any circumstances, fall into enemy hands. If it were discovered that they were not only commandos but also German Jews, there would be no hope of survival. Manfred continues to keep his true identity a secret.

On the evening of 1 July 1944, Manfred is again sent on night patrol. He sets off at dusk with a handful of comrades. With a hedgerow as protection, they look out over the broad fields of the village of Sallenelles, but they can't spy much from this position. Manfred leaves the cover of the hedge and crawls across the open field to get a better look at the German troops. He only gets a few hundred metres before being spotted. Heavy machine-gun fire erupts, and Manfred quickly rolls into a shallow ditch. After a while, the machine-gunning stops, but retreat is no longer an option. As darkness falls, the German soldiers leave their position and head cautiously in his direction. They set up their machine gun a few metres from Manfred's hideout. He can hear their voices, but he can't see them. Several times during the night, a hissing, snake-like sound rings out: Three Troop's signal to make their whereabouts known. Sergeant O'Neill has obviously come back to search for Manfred, but he can't return the call so close to the German soldiers. The search party moves off again. Shortly before daybreak, the German patrol also retreats and, cautiously, Manfred rolls over to the hedge where he'd left his comrades the night before. From there, he slowly moves back to his unit, carefully, so that he doesn't run the risk of being shot at by friendly fire. Once safe and sound with his own men, Manfred doesn't even have time to wash off the black face paint he'd put on for the night patrol: he must report to his superiors immediately. The following is recorded in the troop's war diary:

> On the afternoon of July 1 as a result of exchange of fire between a patrol and the enemy F.D.Ls, Cpl. F. Gray (10 I.A. Cdo. att.) became detached from the patrol. As he had not returned at dusk a search party was sent out to locate him, without success. Cpl. Gray returned early in the morning of July 2, uninjured, having lain up close to the enemy and having gained much useful information. (2 July 1944)

It takes the 41 Commando 10 days to advance from the Orne River to the Seine, 70 kilometres east. Manfred is now the only Three Troop commando in his unit. Maurice Latimer was injured in the battle over the radar station and has been sent back to England for treatment; Tommy Swinton had been suffering intense headaches since D-Day and has also been withdrawn for the time being; and Oscar O'Neill has been assigned to a high-ranking officer back at headquarters. As a Three Troop specialist, Manfred must now accompany almost every patrol and every foray.

Letters from the Front

In September 1944, the 41 Commando finally reaches the port city of Le Havre on the mouth of the Seine. It was from this very place that Manfred's childhood sweetheart Anita set off for a new life six years earlier. Six weeks after D-Day, she receives her first letter from the front:

> I have been wanting to write to you for quite some time, because I think I owe you about half a dozen letters. [. . .]
>
> Well, I am 'somewhere in France' just now, and of course I've been here ever since the game started, so far I've escaped injury (some very narrow escapes too). It's damned difficult to write on anything that's going on here, as it is so very different from the stuff most newspapers try to put across their readers. (24 July 1944)

Manfred is only allowed to divulge details of his whereabouts at least three weeks after the fact, and his letters from the front also pass through the hands of a censor. Nevertheless, he is not shy about sharing his personal impressions and opinions:

> The more I see of the French, the more I like them. The ordinary people seem to have such a lot of grace and intelligence. Normandy is a very fertile province and there was hardly a shortage of food. In the first few days we drank ourselves silly on wine (a thing one can't get anymore in England). Apart from that we captured endless stores of the German Army which they had no time to scorch. Even cars, horses which we put to good uses.
>
> You just can't imagine the destruction that is being caused in this country. Nowadays when a village is being captured great parts of it are just 'flat'. All these lovely

fields are being trampled down, cattle are being killed by
shell and bomb splinters, gardens are being dug up etc. All
this the French take very calmly. I wonder whether they'll
ever be compensated for all this. Quite a lot of them are
being injured and killed. On the second day we were here
I came across a girl of eleven who had a shell splinter in
her hand. It looked a bloody mess. She was crying and
screaming like hell and it was a ghastly experience for me
until I could get her to our M.O. [. . .]

I am sorry this letter is hardly readable, I am not
sitting in a very comfortable writing position. Anyhow I
am getting more illiterate every day. (24 July 1944)

Anita is happy to hear from Manfred and to know that he is doing
well. She also seems quite proud that he is one of the men pushing
the Germans out of France and can hardly wait to learn more.
More than anything, she wants to know what he thinks when he
comes face to face with the 'Jerries'. Manfred replies:

Our feelings towards the Jerries: mixed. If we have gone
'through hell' before getting them we feel like murder or
worse just as a relief, otherwise one takes one cool look
at their eyes and then one usually knows what they are. If
they are decent we may treat them pretty decently [. . .].
The 'fanatics' can easily be recognised: they have a funny
glimmer in their eyes (I know you won't believe that, but
it's true). Generally our attitude is that we despise them
terribly though we can't hate them as that would be an
unbritish attribute. (7 October 1944)

Nearly every day, Manfred and his Three Troop comrades across the armed forces had to face soldiers from the Wehrmacht. In some ways, these young men were very familiar to them; in others, they were utterly alien. In an interview with the BBC from the end of the 1990s, Ian Harris (real name Hans Ludwig Hajos), who was also part of Three Troop, recalls one of these surreal moments. During a night-time sortie, he heard a soldier crying from the German position: 'Mutti, Mutti'. This word and this sound shook Harris to the core: it was exactly what he called his own mother. Cautiously, he moved into the German position and found a large man in an SS uniform lying on the ground, severely wounded. He took his hand and stayed with him until he died.

Manfred had similar experiences. On several occasions, he was detached from his unit at short notice and summoned to a different headquarters to conduct special interrogations through which the British hoped to gather important information. He would then find himself sitting face to face with young German officers. They didn't look that different from him. They were of a similar age and spoke the same language. But they had become his enemies. Manfred could sense fatigue and despair in most of the ordinary Wehrmacht soldiers he encountered, particularly in those who had already fought on the eastern front. Nevertheless, time and time again, he would grow angry when all he heard from them was complaints without an ounce of remorse. One of these interrogations stayed with him for a long time, as he told Anita:

> the other case was the toughest nut I have had as yet: a young fanatical Nazi on some very special job. He didn't actually refuse to talk altogether but he wouldn't

say anything on the things that mattered, only he was not very intelligent so by being hard I could always trick information out of him in a round about way. For three hours I battled my wits against his and I got somewhere where I wanted to get. After I had dismissed him I felt suddenly extremely exhausted. I have never worked myself to such a complete mental standstill and I nearly fell asleep dictating the intelligence report. Looking at this boy's picture of home and girlfriend which I found in his paybook and seeing him often near crying in spite of his terrific self control and in spite of being completely doped with Nazi propaganda, I couldn't help reflecting on the tragedy of it all and I felt very depressed for some time afterwards. (28 December 1944)

None of the Germans seemed surprised that Manfred could speak accent-free German, which in turn surprised him. Although it meant he was not forced to produce his newly fabricated life story, he was a little annoyed that the Germans seemed to consider it self-evident that other people would speak their language perfectly. In any case, his language skills proved an important tool – especially in negotiations on the front. Time and again, situations cropped up in which Manfred and other Three Troop comrades were sent ahead to convince the Wehrmacht officers to surrender. The incentive was simple: every soldier who surrendered was one less soldier they had to fight. They would advance unarmed and make it clear to the Germans that their situation was hopeless, but that, if they gave up their base without a fight, they could hope for fair conditions in British captivity as a prisoner of war. Many of the Wehrmacht officers had already served several gruelling years on the eastern front where they had witnessed heavy losses. They were battle-weary, and most of them acquiesced. Counting all the situations that appear in the Three Troop soldiers' stories and their units' war diaries, Manfred and his comrades were able to convince thousands of soldiers to surrender, which in turn means they indirectly saved countless lives on both sides of the front. These numbers cannot be calculated exactly, but the war diaries of the various units are full of descriptions of courageous, unflinching acts such as this. Of course, these methods were still risky.

Twenty of the Three Troop soldiers would not survive the war. Even the Skipper went missing on D-Day and was presumed dead, although it would later be discovered that he had been severely injured and taken prisoner by the Germans. Manfred learned of these deaths and disappearances when he met up with some fellow Three Troopers in a church in Amfreville a few days after D-Day. On the way there, he passed a newly established military cemetery. Stopping there, he found the graves of George Franklin, born Max Frank; Max Laddy, born Max Lewinsky; and Kenneth William Graham, born Kurt Wilhelm Gumpertz. They were buried beneath a simple white cross. The thought that he, like his comrades, could be buried with a false identity rattled him, and he made up his mind to do something about it. Once a month, Manfred was allowed to write a letter that would not be read by an officer in his unit, but rather screened in the War Office in London where the censors didn't know the soldiers personally – these letters were only assessed for content containing possible military intelligence. Manfred used this opportunity to send a letter through the Wislickis to his younger brother, Theo, asking him to appeal to the Jewish representative of the British Army to take up the issue. The cross was replaced with a Star of David on a few of the graves, but most of the fallen Three Troop soldiers are still buried under a cross to this very day.

Fighting and Faith

In his early letters to Anita from the years 1938 and 1939, Manfred's religion and Jewish identity always played an important role. Then, when he joined Three Troop and took on his new identity, he was required to set aside at least his outward religious practices. Now, on the front, his internal attitude to religion also starts to change. In one of his first letters to Anita from France, he writes:

> Fighting (not war) does of course make a man more religious – if one gets scared stiff (and one is scared stiff nearly all the time) one automatically starts praying. But that's exactly what makes me doubt the truth of religion, it too much looks like a product of fear. Of course I did pray too when we got dive bombed the first time, but then when approaching enemy lines at night – full of 'nerves' – I sometimes do see ghosts too and still they aren't there. Why is it 'not right' to be undecided about such questions nowadays? Surely one can't just make up one's mind, and say this right and this is wrong without having any proofs.
>
> I am pretty idealistic myself and without it I would have never gone in for all this, but my ideal is an 'optimistic realism' and an absolute objectivity. I don't know whether you understand what I mean by that. (24 July 1944)

Anita is worried about Manfred, who seems to be growing colder towards her in his letters. For her, the significance of Jewish religion and identity are only increasing in exile:

> You are right, people fear god more, when they are in danger and they call to him and even talk to him, and after that feel very relieved. But, this does not mean at all that religion is born out of fear, in the contrary, it only emphasizes the fact that everybody believes in Someone above them as it seems that He is the only one they think of at the time of danger. (10 September 1944)

Anita has now been living in New York for six years and, after her initial scepticism, feels at home there. She has built a large circle of friends, almost all of whom are German and Jewish. During the day, Anita earns a small pay cheque working in an office; after work, she goes to evening college, where she is studying English and French. She is still living with her parents in their apartment on the Upper West Side. In the first few years, the family had to share the apartment with two strangers – men from Germany – but they now have it all to themselves, and Anita has her own little room right behind the kitchen. Posters of President Franklin D. Roosevelt, whom she adores, hang on the walls. The room is narrow and hardly gets any daylight, but Anita only spends time here late in the evenings anyway, when she's studying for college or, better yet, writing to Manfred:

> The news coming in over the radio is excellent and hope it, will keep up like this. Boy, oh boy, this would assure us a Victory in 1944. But, I am afraid to be too optimistic

and will just leave it by hoping. I hope you are getting along well. By the way, Fred, do you want to do me a favor? Thanks. Fire for a few shots for me, and you better not miss. For Rosh Hashanah I wish you loads of luck, also to your family. Let us hope and pray that we will find Peace again in the next year. (10 September 1944)

18 September 1944: it is Rosh Hashanah, the Jewish New Year, but there are no celebrations for Manfred. He has spent the day fighting around Dunkirk. In a directive from the start of September, Hitler had designated this French seaport a 'fortress', and 15,000 German soldiers are entrenched there. Only a few hundred Allied soldiers are outside Dunkirk and they cannot take the town. Instead, they launch constant raids to make the Germans believe they are surrounded. During one of these forays, Manfred and his unit are discovered too soon and escape into the city's sewers. So this is where Manfred spends this day of Rosh Hashanah. Even though Manfred is one of the few non-smokers in the army, he smokes one cigarette after another just to bear the stench. He and his comrades manage to return safely to their unit in the darkness of night.

Among all the reconnoitres and raids, Manfred has occasionally got some time off. After two months of continuous service, he was sent to the beaches of Normandy for some R&R, throwing into stark relief how much has changed in such a short time. He describes this somewhat incongruous experience to Anita:

The other day I had a day off from the war, which may sound funny, still that's how it was and it even happens to front line units. A truck took me back the endless way to the beaches and we all went swimming. That part of the French coast has been cleared of mines. It was a lovely day, only the memory of the 'sights' I saw on these beaches on D-Day made the whole experience slightly nauseating. I don't think I'll be capable of spending a holiday in Normandy after the war. There are too many sickening memories. [. . .]

You asked whether I have changed much 'since we first met.' I think the last months have given me a completely different outlook. I have definitely come down to the motto now: 'I've got my food, there is no shelling, therefore I am happy.' One doesn't quite realize in ordinary life what one has got to be thankful for. All the hustling ambitions of life matter not in the least to me now. May be I'll get over that attitude again. (28 August 1944)

Victory Celebrations

In New York, Anita is enjoying a quiet Sunday afternoon. Her final exam is approaching, and books and notepads are lying open in front of her. But Anita can't concentrate. In the background, the radio is broadcasting constant reports from the front. She looks at the large map of the world that hangs above her bed and, while her gaze wanders across the map to Europe, so do her thoughts.

I travel through France and Paris and see the faces of the liberate people, they are all so happy and are so nice to me just because I am an American. In Paris I can still see lots of colored paper lying around, leftovers from their big Armistice Day celebration yesterday. But, the war is not forgotten, and I march on toward Germany and believe it or not, I meet you. 'How do you do!' We are both quite startled and surprised that we should recognize each other. You are well, but I think you could use a good meal, how would a dish of noodle soup, stake with lots of fresh vegetables, a few glasses of fresh milk, a large piece of cake with whipped cream and a delicious cup of coffee, do? I know the combination is not too ingenious, but it tastes good. (12 November 1944)

Paris had already been liberated by Allied forces at the end of August 1944, but only just avoided a disaster. Hitler had decreed that, if Paris fell into enemy hands, all that should be left was a pile of rubble. Disobeying the Führer's orders, the German military commander of the city, Dietrich von Choltitz, surrendered it virtually unscathed.

In the north-east of France, where the 41 Commando is in action, the resistance of the German troops has also been weakening. Manfred is quartered with his unit in a barracks that the Germans have only just left. For the first time in a long time, he has his own small room and a proper bed. A portrait of Hitler is still hanging on the wall. Staring into the eyes of 'that lunatic, looking very burgoisy', he writes a long letter to Anita:

During the last few weeks we have really been made to feel that we are fighting for something worthwhile. The welcome we got everywhere, where we were the first to enter has got to be seen to be believed. Every time we entered a town, flags appeared from I don't know where bands played, churchbells were ringing and huge crowds simply mobbed us. The same scenes everywhere: [. . .] wild scenes of enthusiasm, most excellent victory dinners at night if we stay in the town, living in decent German barracks, left in a hurry instead of living in slit trenches, all that does give you some feeling of greatness. – Mind you, just nothing on earth is a compensation for the other side of war. (9 September 1944)

Though sitting under Hitler's portrait doesn't bother Manfred, Anita is less than impressed:

why do you have to write letters to me under a picture of Der Fuehrer, couldn't you take it down and give it the proper treatment or at least turn it around? (20 October 1944)

Manfred has promised several times to send Anita a present from the front, but he doesn't have a lot of money, and there aren't any shops where he might buy something suitable. Finally, he finds something. Manfred tucks the rank insignia of a German paratrooper he'd arrested and interrogated into a letter. The patch of fabric shows a golden eagle with a swastika. Anita responds:

Thanks for the 'badge', it really was the nices thing you could send me, anything else you can buy would not have pleased me half as much. This badge 'a badge of victory' makes me feel and hope that now we are coming closer to the end of this terrible war and we will then be able to meet, and people all over this world will once more be able to live in peace and happiness. I also want to thank you from the bottom of my heart for fighting for me and us all. (4 December 1944)

The Invasion of Walcheren

After a few relatively quiet weeks, Manfred is about to feel the full force of the war once more. Accompanied by the rest of the 41 Commando and the roar of aeroplanes and battleships, he is involved in another seaborne invasion, this time in Walcheren, a peninsula in the south-west of the Netherlands. With the help of British troops, Antwerp had already been freed in September. The large, and largely undamaged, port in Antwerp was logistically important in the strategy for the upcoming Rhine crossing. So far, though, the Allied fleet has not been able to dock at Antwerp because the Wehrmacht still holds the northern side of the Scheldt estuary. This is about to change.

In the weeks and days leading up to the planned invasion of Walcheren, the Royal Air Force begins a massive aerial attack. The plan is for the bombs to hit the dykes and flood the interior of the peninsula, preventing the Wehrmacht from either getting reinforcements or retreating. The towns and villages of Walcheren are almost completely destroyed by the bombardment and the water rushing in from the ocean. Hundreds of Dutch civilians are killed; thousands lose their homes. But the German troops, sitting in their well-protected bunkers up in the dunes, are hardly affected at all. The construction of the Atlantic Wall had started early in Walcheren, and there are numerous bases and resistance nests dotted along the coast.

Shortly before the invasion, Three Troop commando Maurice Latimer is thrust back into the soldiers' ranks after recovering from his injury. Manfred is reassured: the two of them not only share a similar history, they also completed their elite training together and have total trust in each other.

Operation Infatuate begins at night on 1 November 1944. The invasion of Normandy was in the summer; now, at the beginning of November, it is cold, and this time the Germans are expecting the Allied attack. Manfred is sitting wrapped up on the deck of one of the 100 landing boats. They plough through the grey waters at full speed. Even before they can see land, heavy German artillery fire erupts. Many boats are hit and catch fire. Some even sink. But Manfred's boat manages to avoid damage. The Allies throw smoke grenades to veil the soldiers' landing in a huge cloud, but strong winds quickly disperse the protective haze. They have nearly reached the coast when they hear the drone of dozens of fighter planes rumbling in the sky overhead. At the very same moment, the entire cannon arsenal of the Royal Navy seems to fire at the beaches of Walcheren. Escorted by planes in the air and boats on the water, the troopship carrying Manfred is one of the first to hit the beach. Almost all the amphibious vessels get stuck in the deep sand, but the fire from the German bases briefly falls silent, allowing the soldiers to sprint up the beach where 20 Wehrmacht soldiers are approaching them unsteadily, their hands in the air. The heavy fire from both sea and air has broken their will to fight.

Manfred's unit receives orders to first capture the small city of Westkapelle on the westernmost tip of Walcheren and then advance north to Domburg. The heavy fighting over the peninsula has now been going on for five days. After the daytime offensives, Manfred is also put to work nearly every night. While his comrades are resting, he proceeds to one of the many small makeshift prison camps – it might be a barn on an abandoned farmstead or a captured bunker – to interrogate that day's new prisoners. His task is to obtain information about the next outpost to better prepare them for the following day's attack.

The soldiers of the 41 Commando gain ground faster than anticipated. As their confidence increases, they become less careful. On the sixth day of the invasion, Manfred is injured while marching a few German prisoners off in what he thinks is now a safe area – he doesn't see the German soldiers still hiding nearby, and they are able to launch hand grenades at him. Manfred throws himself to the ground just in time. The explosion mainly injures the German prisoners, but a small piece of shrapnel is embedded in his shoulder. The medic who later treats the wound decides the shrapnel can stay where it is and that Manfred doesn't need to be evacuated. He is, however, assigned to a bed in an empty Dutch house for the night to recuperate a little. Even this night proves short.

At just after 3am on 8 November, Manfred and Maurice Latimer move out, each with a troop of men. They have the last large German base in their sights. Manfred and his fellow commandos manage to sneak just a few metres from the bunker without being made out, and here they sit tight, on standby. In the grey of dawn, they catch the first sound of voices. A huge man steps outside the base with his hands in his pockets and swears at someone to bring him a coffee. Manfred is sure that only a high-ranking officer would behave like this: if he could be captured alive, they would be able to persuade many of the remaining Wehrmacht soldiers in Walcheren to surrender. Manfred is still considering the best course of action when, suddenly, someone leaps at the German officer. It is Maurice, who has approached the base from the other side, obviously with the same idea as Manfred. They are soon able to overpower the Wehrmacht officer and strong-arm him into persuading his soldiers to give in.

Maurice Latimer escorting German prisoners of war, with the Westkapelle lighthouse in the background, 2 November 1944

The days of the nearly five-year German occupation of Walcheren are now numbered. A week after the start of the invasion, negotiations with the peninsula's Wehrmacht commanding generals finally begin; after some hesitation, they agree to surrender. The remaining 3,000 German soldiers are marched off.

At the end of the seven-day battle of Walcheren, Manfred and his comrades bury some of the nearly 500 fallen Allied soldiers in a cemetery in Domburg. Afterwards, the rest of the unit gather in an abandoned cinema in the city, where they go over their experiences of the last few days and allow themselves to celebrate the success of the invasion.

The 41 Commando is sent to De Haan in Belgium. There, the commander of the unit, Colonel Palmer, summons Manfred to his office. Palmer says that he wants to give him a battlefield promotion to the rank of officer. There is just one condition: Manfred must reveal who he really is. On this occasion, Manfred does not hesitate to tell the colonel his story.

After the end of the war, Manfred is nominated for a Bronze Cross, a medal instituted in 1940 by Queen Wilhelmina of the Netherlands while still in exile to honour those who showed bravery or leadership qualities in battle benefiting the Netherlands. The letter of recommendation, now held in the National Archives, summarises that, through Lieutenant Frederick Gray's 'tenacity' and 'complete disregard for personal safety', a lot of useful information could be relayed to the commanding officer. His 'courage and devotion to duty' during the liberation of the Netherlands were extraordinary, it goes on, and he was always a good example to his comrades. A few months after the end of the war, the *London Gazette* announced that Frederick Gray had been awarded the Bronze Cross.

Leave in Brussels

For his efforts in Walcheren, Manfred is granted a two-day furlough. He spends it in Brussels, from where he reports the following to Anita:

what a time I had! [. . .]

The whole town seems to be bent on amusements only, and a soldier grown up in Austerity-Britain must think he is in a dreamland. Cafes-cum cabarets – a thing one has only heard of in Britain –, nightclubs with a fantastic liberty, the amazing good taste in dress, furniture and make-up, dance bands everywhere, shops loaded with stuff (except food) [. . .] still more fantastic is the amount of women everywhere, – no use telling us anything about VD that risk is terribly small compared with other risks one has to take -- but there is not that wild atmosphere of relief after battle. [. . .] It was quite an experience in this life of extremities. [. . .]

All this is one side of the picture. Soon after this 'holiday' I drove through some districts that had seen heavy fighting, where lots of people were homeless. What a misery in this wet and cold winter!! Can you just imagine what people go through when all windows are shattered and there is no glass available? [. . .] I very often ask myself whether this isn't too heavy a prize to pay. If it wasn't bare life itself we are fighting for, I don't know whether it would be worth all this misery. (28 November 1944)

In Brussels, Manfred comes across Jewish civilians for the first time since returning to the European continent. Before the campaign in Walcheren, his Three Troop comrade Robert Geoffrey Hamilton, real name Robert Salo Weich, had given Manfred the address of a Jewish café that he always went to when visiting Brussels. Manfred has barely set foot in the café when a young woman asks him if he knows Robert – Manfred is wearing the same uniform. Manfred answers in the affirmative and explains that it was Robert who had recommended this café to him. And then he steels himself to deliver the bitter news that Robert had fallen in Westkapelle on the first day of the Walcheren landing.

In a letter to Anita, Manfred reflects on the impact of all the death and displacement caused by Hitler's war:

> One meets Jews very rarely out here, but that is mainly because I hardly ever stayed in a big place long enough, to make enquiries about them. The ones one does meet have usually lived in hidings for ages, and very naturally they are utterly disappointed and have adopted a very bitter attitude to life and things in general. I wonder wether they'll get over that?! It is too early to say how many percent of the Jews in Europe survived these last few years; in Belgium it seems to be round 30%, but that is just my estimate and I may be very wrong. (7 December 1944)

The number that Manfred estimated back then – in his typically cool, almost unflappable style – is not quite right. On the eve of the Nazi invasion, there were between 65,000 and 70,000 Jews in Belgium, including many refugees who had poured into the country since the early 1930s. By the war's end, nearly a third of them would be murdered in Nazi concentration camps.

Manfred continues in the same letter:

Antisemitism too is still very wide spread, though in all fairness I don't think one needs to adopt as pessimistic an attitude about it as many people do. By the way that does not mean there are many Jews here who want to emigrate, on the contrary most of the German Jews I met seem to be set even on going back there, arguing that after having survived that ordeal, they'll survive anything, and a bit of antisemitism will just be a minor evil. (This is the sort of attitude we have after going through some very heavy shellfire) (7 December 1944)

Anita is concerned and astonished by what Manfred reports about the Jews in Europe. She is convinced that they shouldn't return to Germany after all the hardships they have been through. Instead, she thinks they deserve a safe country in which they can build a new, carefree life.

Maybe, you will say that it is easy for me to talk that bravely because I am here in America, safe, without many worries, well, that is quite possible, if I were over there I would probably feel different and desperate, but the decision made by a desperate person is never, or hardly ever, the right one. But, why do I tell you all that? It will not change anything, I suppose I just want you to know how I feel about all this, and I assure you that I feel very, very strongly for these people, they are one of us and that link cannot be broken. (10 January 1945)

The End of the War Draws Near

On 3 December 1944, Manfred's promotion is officially approved. It has taken a little under four years for this enemy alien to become an officer of the British Army. Manfred now has access to the officer's mess and is happy about his new clothes and better bed. Above all, he is now able to enjoy a warm bath for the first time since leaving England six months ago. It tickles his vanity, even if he often emphasises in his letters that he actually finds the whole hierarchy of the military very suspect. The return address on his envelopes now shows 'Lieutenant Frederick Gray' and he can now compose his letters on a typewriter, like Anita, who mostly writes to Manfred late in the evenings from her little room in Manhattan:

It is one o'clock at night but it does not matter tonight, since I can sleep as long as I want to tomorrow. Yes, that's right it is Christmas and although, we do not celebrate this holiday at home, it does remind you of lots of beautiful things. It means happiness and joy in every house, song and laughter. All this exists here, most families are happy have their big dinner parties and a tall and well decorated Christmas tree, but all this gaiety is not quite complete, as a matter of fact, it is rather artificial. They all miss their sons, brothers, husbands and sweethearts and only after the war, joy, a complete joy, can again be in the hearts of all. [. . .]

I am sorry, dear, for talking so much about the war, I know you don't like it so much, you have enough of it without my letters, so I better snap out of my blue modd – a very frequent mood of mine – and talk about something else. What are you doing right now? I wonder, I do hope you are behind the lines and are having a good time. (24 December 1944)

At the end of 1944, for the first time since entering the war, Manfred is not stationed near the front and is, in fact, having a good time. He is quartered for a few weeks in a barracks near Middelburg, where he has his own room with an electric light, which, to his great surprise, even works for a few hours during the day. There is no fighting in the area, but there are other urgent assignments: he is working as an interpreter with the Royal Engineers of the British Army and a few members of the Dutch civilian population to support plans to rebuild the dykes. Having grown up close to the border and as the son of a German–Dutch family, he has been familiar with the language of this neighbouring country since childhood.

The vast stretches of flooded land on Walcheren have frozen in the cold December days. Manfred acquires a pair of skates from a farming family and, late in the evenings, goes ice skating under the moonlight. These are silent and peaceful nights. On 28 December, he writes to Anita: 'That's life at its best and by god do I appreciate that now!' Had Anita been able to read these lines immediately, it might well have brightened her mood. Anita has left New York for a few days to go skiing with some friends in the Catskill Mountains. Every year when she was young, she and her parents had decamped from Berlin to the Swiss Alps for the winter break, and she loves skiing. But she is unable to fully enjoy it. Why should she of all people have such an untroubled life? On New Year's Eve, she tells Manfred, she will sneak out just before midnight, as has become her habit. She would rather spend the start of the year alone, thinking of her old friend than be with her new American acquaintances.

> If you are not really together with the people you want to be with is ti not better to imagine they are with you then to force yourself to have a good time with those you don't care for. (24 December 1944)

Manfred will also be a guest at her imaginary New Year's party, she assures him in her letter. In reality, Manfred sees 1945 in with Andrew Kershaw, real name Andre Kirschner, a friend from Three Troop who had shown up in his unit a few days before. Both leave the officers' party early as they don't feel like getting drunk with the entire squad. They pour themselves a glass of whisky and listen to Hitler's New Year's address on the radio in silence. While thousands of bombs are falling right across Germany on New Year's Eve 1944, Hitler is bombarding the nation with his unwavering faith in a resounding victory. These hollow words are just background noise for Manfred. Later, he describes to Anita that he and Andrew were lost in their own thoughts:

> Well we both knew what the other was thinking. Our thoughts were not with the loved ones so far away though they may have entered through a side door – we were just thinking 'Are we going to overlive this year or all those horrible things going to happen to us that we

have seen happening to the bodies of other people friend and foe alike? Our thoughts must have moved pretty much alike for suddenly we both said rather sarcastically 'Well, here's to us'. (31 March 1945)

At the start of 1945, Manfred goes back to England for the first time since D-Day. Now that he is an officer, and since his unit is no longer stationed directly on the front, he has been delegated to train young recruits for a few weeks. In mid-March, well-rested and in good spirits, he returns to his unit in the Netherlands, which is now stationed at Goes – not that far from the town where his parents were last in hiding prior to their deportation. Having had neither time off nor leads, he has been unable to do anything until now and is anxious to find out what has become of them. Perhaps there are surviving relatives in Amsterdam who know something? Or maybe he can find clues through the Dutch authorities? Amsterdam has not yet been liberated, though, and his unit is still being kept in Goes. The advance into Germany is another thing he can only follow from a distance. From where he is stationed, he can see enormous wings of Allied aircraft flying east, which are carrying thousands of paratroopers to the other side of the Rhine. Only later will he discover that his cousin Herbert Jonas is among them. They grew up together in Borken, and Herbert is now fighting in Germany as a US soldier.

My dear Anita,

I could just sit down and cry; there is the British Second Army driving into my home country (Borken fell yesterday) and here am I sitting in a so-called 'quiet sector' doing just about nothing like the rest of the chaps of my unit. 'Eating our heads off'. It is annoying. [. . .] Nevertheless I got permission to push off and have a look at the old places one of the next few days. (30 March 1945)

Just one day after writing these lines, the time has arrived. It is 31 March 1945 and it is Pesach, the Jewish festival celebrating the Israelites' liberation from slavery and flight from Egypt. Together with his friend Andrew Kershaw, Manfred crosses the Rhine and returns to Borken for the first time in seven years: 'This definitely was one of the most interesting days I have had in the army,' he tells Anita.

Manfred has seen a lot in the last few months, but what awaits him on the other side of the Rhine shocks him nonetheless. Practically everything has been destroyed: 'Germany 1945 Style' is his succinct description. Now that they are on German soil, the Allies have changed their strategy. To minimise civilian casualties during the liberation of France, British units always engaged in urban warfare that involved heavy military losses; now they are using a different strategy: if the Germans surrender cities without a fight, they are mostly spared artillery fire. But there is no holding back from the air. To ensure that the advancing infantry meets as little resistance as possible, the cities directly across the Rhine see a particularly heavy amount of bombing in the final weeks of the war, including Borken on 23 March 1945. Nearly all the houses in the centre are now burnt out and collapsed. Although Manfred and Anita have written exclusively in English since resuming their correspondence, he switches back to his mother tongue when he tells her: 'It does one a great deal of good to see that the old school got a direct hit.'

Borken city centre, 1945

Manfred stops the jeep at his school and walks down Bocholter Straße. Old Mrs Dirding is working in front of her house, as if she has been doing nothing else for the last seven years. He also recognises Mr Flecke and that elderly lady that his teacher Mr Locker used to live with. Manfred does not shy away from being recognised by them, but neither does he seek it out. The British Army has just set up its headquarters in Manfred's family home. He steps into the house he grew up in.

> Gosh it was funny getting back into the old place! I did think of you quite a lot whilst I was there. Again and again I met people whom I recognized, I don't know wether they recognized me. (2 April 1945)

In his lines can be heard a certain satisfaction at returning as a victor to this town that had previously cast him out. He looks on sceptically at the first measures taken by the Military Government. His comrades seem to have no idea how to issue unambiguous orders to the Germans. It bothers him that important decrees, such as the dissolution of the National Socialist Party or the reintroduction of press freedom, are being posted in front of the headquarters in writing that is much too small, in German that is much too complicated.

When Anita reads about Manfred's trip to Borken, it stirs up memories for her too:

> Freddie, do you know that it is exactly 7 years now that we have not seen each other. I left your house on the 4th of July in the morning. I remember everything as clearly as if it was only yesterday, the days at your house, then Brussels, Paris, Le Havre, the trip and finally the USA, yes, these were eventful days for me. (3 July 1945)

Anita is sorry that Manfred couldn't be part of capturing Borken himself, but assures him that the invasion of every German city will offer satisfaction.

On 12 April 1945, President Roosevelt suddenly dies. It is something the world had not anticipated. Anita is stunned and is still mourning the loss a few days later. Roosevelt has been an important role model for her and is her ideal of a good politician. To the same extent that she worships Roosevelt, she despises Hitler. In her letters, she expresses malice towards him at almost every opportunity:

> Tomorrow is Hitler's last birthday. I hope he will 'celebrate' it accordingly. I can just imagine that the RAF is sending him several packages by airmail. (19 April 1945)

It is not Royal Air Force bombs that take Hitler's life, though; he does it himself on 30 April, a few days after his birthday.

Since the end of the war started drawing into sight, Manfred and Anita have increasingly been discussing where and how the Jews of Europe will live. Anita writes about a friend from Germany who is now living in Palestine. This friend's enthusiasm for the country makes an impression on Anita, and she shares the conviction that the young generation will establish something new there, 'even if they have to fight for it'. She thinks that Manfred shouldn't give up the hope of Jewish people living in the world in safety and that Palestine could offer a chance. He tells Anita that he still has his doubts:

> I don't think at all it is possible to sit down and say 'now let us find a solution once and for all'. No country affords security from antisemitism [. . .] and one can't exactly say that Palestine offers a peaceful and socially and economically secure haven. No, in my opinion a highly insecure life has to be accepted not only by the Jews but by nearly everybody. (11 February 1945)

Anita vehemently disagrees with Manfred. Life may be uncertain – it could hardly be recognised as being otherwise – but she will not accept this as an 'incorrigible evil':

> I feel, just because life offers so little security, certainty, we should try everything and not leave one stone unturned to make it safe and secure. Probably it will be

without success as the past can show, but still I refuse to give up the struggle. Because what else is there to life for but happiness and what is happiness but a state of well-being and security.

Rereading this last paragraph, I feel that I must have misunderstood your letter, or rather you must have written it in a rather disgusted mood, as I am quite convinced that you will agree with me. Or have you changed, has the war changed your outlook on life? (9 March 1945)

Manfred's attitude has indeed changed. In Borken, and in his time in England, he kept the company of various groups influenced by Zionism. Now, he writes to Anita:

I have my grave doubts now wether the whole thing is fair to the Arabs. If we believe in Democracy I doubt if we have the right to *force* our opinions on them and without their goodwill (which we might be able to get) our methods are rather those of intruders. (5 May 1945)

There had always been a Jewish community living in Palestine. It grew from the 1880s onwards in the wake of the pogroms in Russia and the emerging Zionist movement, whose goal was the return of the Jews to 'Eretz', the area of biblical Israel. After 1933, and especially after the November pogrom of Kristallnacht in 1938, more and more Jews from central Europe rushed to Palestine. Despite the increasing pressure for emigration from Europe, Britain did not increase the immigration quotas – fearing it would escalate the already smouldering conflict with the country's Arab population – and Prime Minister Churchill, who had originally been sympathetic to the Zionist movement, distanced himself from the idea of a Jewish 'home' in Palestine under the influence of both anti-Zionist and antisemitic voices in the British gentry.

In the East

Meanwhile, Manfred is still in Goes, and still doesn't know anything about his parents' fate. Anita has asked about it repeatedly, but he has never answered. Then, shortly before the end of the war, he receives a letter from a relative in New York. Manfred has not heard from her in years.

> Dear Manfred,
>
> yesterday arrived a letter from Mr. [Elzas], Grand Hotel Montreux, Switzerland, saying that he spent the past 5 months with your parents in [Theresienstadt,] that they are in good health and spirit [. . .]. Is that good news – my boy, or? [. . .]
>
> Hope you are feeling better after reading that letter. We all did for sure. [. . .]
>
> Keep well – my very best regards
>
> yours
>
> Erna Edith Beihoff (1 April 1945)

The Swiss politician Jean-Marie Musy had conducted secret negotiations with the Reichsführer of the SS, Heinrich Himmler, and succeeded in having prisoners released from Theresienstadt in exchange for millions of francs. Musy was negotiating on behalf of Jewish organisations in Switzerland and the USA, who provided the funds necessary for the liberation. In February 1945, 1,200 prisoners were able to leave the camp for Switzerland. More were supposed to follow, but when Hitler learned of the secret deal between Himmler and Musy, he forbade any further ransoming of concentration-camp inmates. Among the 1,200 who arrived in Switzerland on the first transport was Hermann Elzas, an acquaintance of the Gans family. Now that he was safe and free, he was able to pass on his knowledge of their whereabouts.

After being deported from Camp Westerbork to Bergen-Belsen in the autumn of 1943, Manfred's parents were held there for nearly six months. Moritz had lost a leg fighting for the German Empire in the First World War and, since then, had worn a prosthesis from the knee down. Neatly rolled up in a little cavity in his wooden leg, he hid not only his diary, but also a slip of paper. In large letters on the oversized letterhead was written 'Reichsverband deutscher Kriegsopfer e.V.' Moritz Gans had become president of the Borken branch of the Reich Association of War Disabled in the 1920s – until he was told in 1933, through this very letter, that he was being expelled. The letter turned out to be a blessing in disguise: by way of thanks for his loyal service, it assured him of the association's protection. The letter states: 'Please notify us immediately of any actions against you or your family by unauthorised persons. Heil Hitler!' With great foresight that this letter might one day prove useful, Moritz had kept it. And he was right: ten years later, he and Else were not sent from Bergen-Belsen on a train to Auschwitz, which presumably would have delivered them directly to the gas chambers, but were instead taken in transport number XXIV/3 to a camp in Theresienstadt, near Prague.

In 1943, tens of thousands of Jews arrived in Theresienstadt from Germany, Austria, the Netherlands and Denmark. Among them were many older people who had once held senior positions, as well as prominent actors, athletes, musicians and writers – all considered 'privileged' Jews in the Nazi logic of selection. As a disabled and decorated veteran of the First World War, Moritz was added this group.

Only much later would Manfred read what his father Moritz wrote in his little diary at the time:

Anything that can move must travel 3 km on foot to the train station, young and old. At the station (loading platform) stand 7 freight cars with straw on the ground. Our people throw the suitcases aimlessly and haphazardly into the carriages, hurried on by the SS with curses and kicks. I climb from the wagon with my chair and haversack, search as best I can for our suitcases and blankets, throw them into the corner of a carriage and save a spot for Else next to me. Our age group is arriving now; everyone is making a dash for the carriages, so I call out to Else. She jumps up and sits on the blanket next to me. The carriage is full to bursting. Fifty-nine people and lots of luggage; many are standing, unable to sit. And now the terrible thing: the air vents are closed, nailed shut from the outside, and now the doors are closed completely, too. With the SS laughing scornfully, the train pulls out. We cannot imagine that the chosen and privileged Jews would be sent to Theresienstadt like this and still think that the train will only be shunted and then we will be able to open the cattle car's door or air vents. No light, no water, no bucket for our needs: this is how 375 people are sent on a journey that will take 3 days and 2 nights. What we suffered in these days and nights is something I don't want to describe. Our carriage leader (Manfred Greifenhagen) held himself splendidly: at least everyone sat down; no one was allowed to stand the whole time, and this is how no one in our carriage went mad. (27 January 1944)

During the journey, Moritz bored a small hole in the iron air vent with a can opener. Through this, he could catch glimpses of the outside world and tell the other people in the cattle car what he could see as the train headed towards the camp.

I saw a city with tall houses and outside in the fields and on the streets where we were travelling, only people with Stars of David. [. . .] Then we stopped on a street between the houses. After a while, the doors were ripped open and we were standing in the light. It was good that you couldn't see yourself, for we must have looked awful. (27 January 1944)

Without exchanging a word, Moritz and Else threw down their few possessions and climbed out of the wagon. They were ordered to leave everything where it was and immediately line up in rows of five. Moritz recognised some acquaintances from Camp Wester-bork, and they called out a few words to him. He examined their tired faces as they dragged themselves past. Could this really be Theresienstadt, the city of 'Jewish self-administration' where the Nazis claimed elderly Jews were sent for retirement? Moritz whispered to Else: 'We are in a ghetto.'

They were led to the 'sluice', where an SS guard told them to strip and hand over all their belongings and that anyone who tried to hide private possessions would have death to reckon with. After being searched, they were registered by Jewish camp inmates.

While Theresienstadt was controlled by the SS and guarded by Czech gendarmes, a Jewish self-administration was burdened with the complex and gruelling organisation of camp life. It was the inmates themselves who allocated rooms, distributed food and assigned and oversaw the work. They also compiled lists for the transports further east. The prisoners in Theresienstadt may have administered their own lives, but they did not determine them – they had no real influence over their fate and were constantly subjected to the despotism of the SS.

Moritz and Else were put in separate accommodation and assigned work duties. Moritz would repair shoes and Else would work in the fields. They could see each other in the afternoons and evenings, when they would comfort each other and reminisce. In the first few months after their arrival, Moritz hardly wrote anything in his carefully hidden diary. On 8 July, there is a brief entry: 'We are celebrating our silver wedding.' How exactly they celebrated, Moritz did not say. The sorrow of losing the world they lived in, concern over the whereabouts of their children, fear at every new transport further east, the strain of their work and, above all, permanent hunger were their constant companions over the months to come.

Not long after receiving the news from the US that his parents are in the Theresienstadt ghetto, Manfred writes a letter to Anita over a few days:

> Peace-roumors are chasing about again and perhaps by the time you get this it is really all over, though I personally can't quite think how. [. . .] Horrors in the concentration camp are another topic, as if we hadn't known. (29 April 1945)
>
> My parents are at the moment in Theresienstadt in Czechoslovakia and I am looking forward to a trip there. It's all laid on from this side I only hope the blasted Russians won't make any difficulty, they seem to get in for Red tape in a still larger way than we do. (5 May 1945)

Manfred writes a short note on the back of the envelope before sending it to Anita: 'Hurrah it's over on this front. Just received the news.'

In the early morning of 7 May 1945 at the headquarters of the Allied forces in Reims, Colonel General Alfred Jodl, on behalf of the German High Command, signs an unconditional surrender, which would come into effect on 8 May. In the coming hours and days, Allied soldiers and civilians from the liberated countries celebrate. But for Manfred, it is not yet over: he has received permission from his superior to go on his own mission.

On 12 May, four days after the capitulation, he sets off.

Chapter Six

May 1945

Only a few hours have passed since Manfred and his driver left their base. They have gathered so many impressions along the way that the 200 kilometres they've put behind them feel like a trip halfway around the world. Despite a few hitches, they've already made it to Borken. After this small detour to see the family home again, the plan is to get to Theresienstadt as quickly as possible. Manfred only has overview maps of Germany and Czechoslovakia in his rucksack, each dating from before the war; apart from this, they don't know which of the roads and highways will even be navigable now. Bit by bit, Manfred and his driver Bob must find their own way. For the next stage, though, Manfred doesn't need any map at all. They travel down familiar roads from Borken to Münster, where he wants to get rid of the two Canadians they've picked up.

British troops have assumed command in Borken and the surrounding villages, but they run into the US Army just a few kilometres down the road. The soldiers are sitting in front of their quarters looking bored. Manfred asks his driver to stop for a moment so he can talk to a few of the US soldiers. Now that the war is over, they all just want to know when they will get to go home. For his part, Manfred wants to know what state the region is in. 'It's lousy during the day, but we do alright at night,' answers a sergeant, grinning.

They reach Münster in the early evening and head for the US Army HQ. They ask whether they can stay for the night. The Yankees allocate him a bed in the officers' quarters. When he gets there, he realises that the building he's been sent to was once part of a German barracks. He remembers as a boy standing outside the gates of precisely these barracks and looking on enviously at the German soldiers drilling in the courtyard. Now, just under ten years and half a lifetime later, he is sitting between gum-chewing Americans, tired but happy, with the insignia of the Royal Marines on his shoulder. There is coffee and doughnuts. Manfred gets into conversation with the Yanks. In the travel report he will make on 20 May 1945, after his return, he notes:

> Everyone is full of how they are being teased by the German
> girls when then go swimming. 'Allow us to rape them or
> shoot them' they demand, 'we can't go on like this.'

When the Allies invaded, the Americans and British enacted a 'non-fraternisation order', which meant that their soldiers were forbidden any 'private' relationship with German men, women or children. Even now that the Wehrmacht has capitulated, the commanders still fear counterattacks through the German underground movement *Werwolf*, whose members might pretend to be friendly in order to gain sensitive information. The Allied army's radio stations and newspapers are constantly broadcasting warnings that pretty girls could sabotage Allied victory and that smart

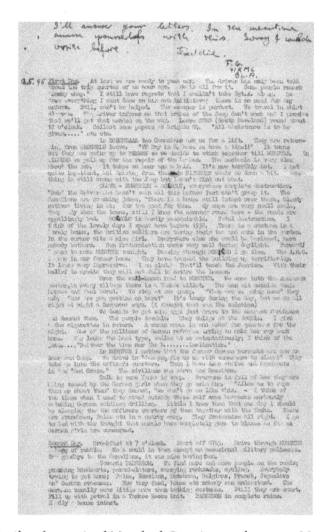

Facsimile of page 1 of Manfred Gans's travel report, May 1945

soldiers don't fraternise. The social distance is also supposed to make it clear to the Germans that they are not victims of the war; they share the blame for their own suffering.

The US soldiers tell Manfred that the French, Polish and other units stationed nearby fraternise with the enemy to their heart's content; only the Americans and Brits are complying with the orders, which only serves as an act of self-punishment. Since the end of the war in Europe, if not before, though, the prohibition on fraternisation has started being observed less and less, and the Allied soldiers' interest in German women is now enormous. Manfred writes in his report that he went to bed thinking that 'morals have completely gone to blazes as far as German girls are concerned'. The country he is travelling through strikes him as simultaneously familiar and strange. At times, the uninhibited, crude demeanour of some of the Allied soldiers seems just as foreign to him.

Early the next morning, Manfred bids farewell to his Canadian companions, who plan to take the road to Bremen, and he and Bob set off eastwards just after 7am. Manfred has passed through countless gutted towns and villages in the last ten months, but the extent of the destruction in Münster is beyond anything he has ever seen before. The city centre has been hit with 700,000 bombs. All that remains of the magnificent old gabled houses that Manfred recalls from his youth is debris. Lone steel joists and the beams of burnt-out, crumbling roof trusses rise up from the wreckage like the bones of a cadaver. The many church towers have been shorn off, and the few figures moving through the city seem broken and confused. British Army machinery has cleared away the worst of it from the main roads, but many side streets can still only be recognised as narrow tracks between mountains of rubble. Bob slowly manoeuvres the jeep along the bumpy roads. Outside the city walls, a completely different scene soon opens up in front of them.

Exodus

May 1945 is sunny and warm. The trees are lush and green, and the sky hasn't been this bright and blue for what feels like an eternity.

Between the ruins, apple trees are blooming. But the most peaceful thing about these days is the silence: no grenades, no aerial attacks, no sirens. An odd calm after the storm is spreading across the land.

While the cities have been reduced to rubble, the rural areas are often astoundingly undamaged. In the fields, the crops are unusually tall for this time of year. Millions of forced labourers were made to slave away on farms to ensure agricultural yields. Until shortly before the end of the war, this meant that Germany had more food than people in the countries they invaded. Even after the end of the war, when hunger reaches the ruined cities, supplies in the countryside are comparatively good. Those who have been bombed flock to the surrounding farmsteads asking for food.

Manfred and his driver are hungry, too, and stop at the next farmhouse. They don't have to ask – they just demand a few eggs. As Manfred describes in his travel report, their uniforms and the tommy guns slung over their shoulders are persuasion enough:

> The people tremble. They oblige at the double. I give a few cigarettes in return. A woman comes in and asks for quarters for the night. One of the millions of German refugees.

As soon as the war ended, a mass migration of almost inconceivable proportions began. Millions of people are now streaming in every direction. Displaced people from the east move west in small convoys, hoping to find relatives, friends and a new home. They push handcarts and prams or carry their worldly possessions in sacks over their shoulders. Some have bicycles. Only a few find a seat on a horse-drawn cart. Most of them are driven only by their feet and the hope of finding a fresh start somewhere soon.

Those who were deported by the Nazi regime have even less. The National Socialists abducted prisoners of war and civilians from all the occupied territories and brought them to the Reich to fill the holes in industry and agriculture left by the mobilisation of German men. Ten million people who survived forced labour and malnourishment are now making their way back home. Some of them are still wearing prison clothes; others the tattered uniform of the army they had served in. Weak and undernourished, they have emerged in recent days from farms, factories and mines, looking for the quickest way out of the country of their tormentors. Mostly, they are headed east.

In the other direction, bewildered and traumatised, come returning German soldiers who have been able to flee the Russian advance in the east and are now seeking their old lives. The pride with which some of them once donned their German army uniform has vanished.

Germany in May 1945: massive confusion surrounded by almost endless destruction. Every street lays the catastrophe bare. The roads are lined with innumerable shot-up, burnt-out German military vehicles and the bodies of dead soldiers. The living limp past. Columns of defeated Wehrmacht soldiers face columns of American and British troops. In moments of confusion, German officers tentatively salute the victors. Elsewhere, concentration-camp survivors come across SS guards – victims and perpetrators constantly cross paths in these days.

From his jeep, Manfred looks into the many faces in amazement. Men and women, boys and girls, practically all the peoples of Europe are passing silently by, their expressions hungry and empty.

Everybody trying to get home; Poles, Russians, Dutchmen, Belgians, French, Jugoslavs and German evacuees. How they feed, house, etc. nobody can understand. [. . .] But the great sight of the Autobahn is 'Europe going home.' It's like an Exodus. There are just millions on the roads.

Mostly they drag themselves through the country with their heads sunk, resentful, sorrowful or simply exhausted. But rays of sunshine spark the growth of a delicate green over piles of rubble and a twinkle in the eyes of a few. Some people manage to raise their heads, relax their tunnel vision and find expression for the almost imperceptible shift in these days between downfall and new beginnings. Diary entries and letters from spring 1945 testify to the utterly contradictory emotions many are feeling: sorrow for the people who have been lost, concern over those who are still missing and, despite everything, relief at being alive. At the same time, there is the suspicion that the effects of the last few years' events will continue to be felt for decades to come. The horror of what happened and the hope for redemption are intertwined.

Not far from Manfred's route, the young German writer Wolfgang Borchert is travelling up from the south. 'Come, darling May, and make the graves green again,' he calls out. Borchert, a Wehrmacht soldier just a few months older than Manfred, had managed to escape while being transported to a French prison and is now struggling to walk the 600 kilometres back north to Hamburg. Once there, he initially grapples with speechlessness, but finds his voice again and puts the instability of his generation down on paper in 1947 in *On the Move – Generation without Farewell*:

> We meet in the world as man and man – and then we steal away, for we are without ties, without resting-place and without farewell. We are a generation without farewell, stealing away like thieves, because we are afraid of our heart's cry. We are a generation without homecoming, for we have nothing we could come home to, and we have no one to take care of our hearts – so we have become a generation without farewell and without homecoming.

Coming from the east, another young Wehrmacht soldier is on his difficult journey home. Claus Hubalek, who is later to become the head dramaturg of Northern German Broadcasting and the Hamburg Theatre, served in the Luftwaffe in the last few months of the war; now, at the beginning of May, he is on his way back to Berlin. While Manfred looks on at the scenes of May 1945 through the eyes of a victor, Claus Hubalek describes his complete shock at what he was seeing in *Unsre jungen Jahre. Tagebuch eines Zwanzigjährigen* (1947):

> I allow myself to be carried along in the stream of people. Once we are out of the village, we hear a high buzzing sound. 'Hedge hopper!' a woman calls out, and everyone presses themselves to the ground. The first bursts of fire are already hacking into the pavement. A child screams. People are moaning. Just no more death now, just stay

alive now. A woman is lying in front of me. Her sack of flour has burst open, and the street is decked in white. A thin red streak eats its way into the flour. When the planes have passed, a soldier bends over the woman. He raises her arm, which falls back down to the pavement limply. 'She's finished.' He looks at me with gaping eyes. 'Let's see what she's got on her.' He rummages through the woman's pockets, pulls out boxes of biscuits, a packet of butter, cigarettes. The carton is bloody. He carefully wipes the blood away with his sleeve, laughs and tears the carton open. Slowly, he lights a cigarette. He looks down at the woman again and walks away, whistling.

Just past Kassel, Manfred and Bob turn onto the southward-bound Reichsautobahn. They can travel more quickly here. The sun is still burning in the sky and the jeep's engine is running hot. They cut the motor whenever they go downhill. It's better this way. But then they notice that a spring has broken. They find a US barracks in Eisenach. Everyone is very surprised to see British soldiers so far east. The American mechanic is not exactly thrilled at Manfred and Bob's request, but Manfred manages to persuade him to take a quick look at his 'Willys', as the American and British jeeps were called in the Second World War. After an hour, a new spring has been fitted and they can set off again.

From Eisenach, they travel through Gotha to Weimar. At the cloverleaf interchange, where the east–west autobahn meets the north–south one, they are checked by American military police. It is the only time they have been stopped so far. Manfred shows the letter from his superior and they are waved through.

No matter who he talks to now, the 'Line of Contact' – the demarcation between the territories controlled by the Americans and the Russians – is always the first thing that comes up.

Even before the end of the war, the Russians, Americans and English – and later also the French – had divided Germany up into different occupation zones. But in these first post-war days, everything still needs to be ironed out. Often, it is not clear where exactly the borders are and who is allowed to cross them. Manfred is worried that they may run into some kind of military regulation at some point that could prevent them continuing. All they can do is feel their way forwards, bit by bit.

Towards CHEMNITZ now, it is getting cooler. There are more Yankee patrols on the roads, but of course the Yanks and Russians only met in DRESDEN according to information. We'll stay in CHEMNITZ and make enquiries there whether THERESIENSTADT is American or Russian and what the chances are to get through the Russian lines. [. . .]

Here is CHEMNITZ, white flags everywhere 5 or 6 at every house. Why? has the place only just been taken? There are no soldiers on the streets. Where is all the Yankee transport? Perhaps it's too late in the day. The Germans look at us in amazement. Wonder whether the place has been taken yet??! Suddenly a lot of Russian soldiers. They don't look like ex-prisoners to me. No, they have got weapons. The famous Russian tommy gun! Gosh! we are in their lines already. Damn! A crowd of Cossacks in front of us. They wave wildly. That's better. Two officers ride up on horse back. They look grim. Silently they shake hands with us. I try my French. One understands. I look at him. He seems to be Jewish. 'Seien sie a Jid?' 'A Jid, a Jid he shouts.' I ask him for the nearest American soldiers. He points in one direction. Slaps me on the back then we all salute and I ride away.

A few kilometres further on, Manfred and his driver must stop again. Two wires are stretched across the street. Two armed soldiers are standing side by side: an American and a Russian. 'We get on fine,' says the last American sentinel before the Russian-controlled zone: 'They come to us to loot from the Germans because we don't do it so thoroughly, and we go to them because we can "fraternize". [. . .] The "line" only exists for German soldiers and civilians.' Manfred enquires about the nearest US headquarters – he wants to gather more information about what he can expect in the east and also wants a letter written in Russian in his pocket. The American points the way to the US Company HQ in Oberlungwitz. Without being asked, the Russian lowers the wires strung across the street and lets the British jeep drive back into the American zone.

Oberlungwitz is a small industrial town between Chemnitz and Zwickau. The US Colonel George C. Clowes and his troops have requisitioned a stylish villa at the edge of town. Until he was forced to vacate it for the Americans, it had been the home of Mr Götze, an industrialist who owns several artificial silk factories and lots of property in the area. When Manfred reaches the building, he finds a group of German refugees gathered there, all asking for help. The colonel shoos them away, but they show no signs of leaving. Only when he pulls out his pistol demonstratively does the crowd dissolve. Now Manfred has the chance to put his request to the colonel in peace. He agrees to organise the letter, but invites Manfred to stay a night; it is too late to drive on. Manfred accepts the invitation gratefully.

> It is the most modern comfortable and luxurious building I have ever seen. [. . .] My driver and myself have a bath. Marble bathrooms. It is too good to be true. [. . .] When I come down again a meal is waiting. Just now Churchill starts his speech on the wireless. I listen whilst having my food. Gosh! I am hungry. That American Colonel is terrific, so are his officers.

Although it is now 10pm, Oberlungwitz HQ is still bustling. The colonel and a few of his officers sit with Manfred. Instead of being left to relax, Manfred is drawn into a lively discussion. The main topic is the Russians: 'What a queer crowd,' they say.

> 'They have no system at all of how to treat the Germans.' 'They never give the Germans a chance.' 'I had a look at their weapons, they are good, but I still think we can beat them; if we don't do it now we'll have to do it in ten years, and then they'll be producing their own transport.' [. . .] I try to argue with them. We must not judge them by our standards.

Every day, German refugees and prisoners of war arrive in Oberlungwitz from the Russian-controlled zone. Word has long been circulating that there is more to the Americans than just chocolate and Lucky Strikes; they are more lenient with German POWs and civilians. In comparison, the Red Army is preceded by a frightening reputation, fuelled by its actual violence and years of Nazi propaganda, which never missed an opportunity to paint the Russians as vindictive, predatory barbarians.

Late in the evening, news comes in that another 3,000 German refugees are expected the next morning. The Americans only assumed control of the town a few days ago, and providing for these people will present a great challenge. Colonel Clowes wants to go down to Mr Götze's abandoned factory to find out if the kitchen there is still working. He asks Manfred to come along and interpret.

> Herr Gotz is dressed in a very well cut suit. He leads us around. Then we start discussing things. [. . .] [The] subject switches to politics. Now he shouts at the top of his voice and gesticulates, 'I tell you Stalin has won the war – he cries – here under your very nose the local Bürgermeister published an order that nobody is to get any food who doesn't belong to the Free German Party. He is a Communist.' 'We go from one extreme into the other.' 'Our people have lost everything, they'll become Communists.' The Colonel says, 'I am afraid so.' Gotz cries, 'How can Europe be healthy?' 'Two wars in every generation.' I remind him that it usually was Germany who started them.
>
> 'My children shall not stay in Europe, even if I lose millions.' For everything I have an answer so he gets annoyed. 'You are far too young, I can't talk with you.' That gets me annoyed. I start fumbling with my pistol.

He doesn't like it. We leave him and go back. The Yanks say, 'He is right somehow.' I don't agree.

Back at HQ, Manfred and the colonel drink another few glasses of wine. It is late at night when Manfred finally falls into bed in a nursery in the Götze Villa. Mother's Day – 13 May 1945 – is drawing to a close. Will he see his parents again tomorrow?

After a short night, a hefty 'Yankee breakfast' is waiting for Manfred and his driver. Soon after breakfast they want to get going, but they have barely got into the jeep when they are again besieged by German refugees asking how they can get their property from behind the Russian lines. Manfred tells them that they started the war with Russia. 'The Nazis did,' they respond. Manfred and Bob finally chase them away with riding whips.

Manfred doesn't have any more time for other people's requests and sensitivities. The jeep is checked again. The Americans fill up the tank for him and give him a large box of provisions. The colonel presents Manfred with a letter in Russian that should guarantee safe passage.

The Allies' sphere of influence ends at the foot of the Ore Mountains. This last section will be the thorniest part of the route. Every kilometre east takes them into more dangerous territory. But if Manfred wants to get to Theresienstadt, he has no choice but to continue.

Hope and Fear

Moritz and Else Gans have endured Theresienstadt for more than a year now.

Since being established in 1941, the camp took on various functions in the context of the Nazi policy of extermination. Initially, Theresienstadt was a collection and transit camp – similar to Westerbork – for the Jews from the 'Protectorate of Bohemia and Moravia', as the occupied territories of Czechoslovakia were called by the Nazi state. Then, from 1942, Jews from the 'Greater German Reich' also started being incarcerated there. The Nazi regime made many propagandist claims about Theresienstadt, describing it as a model Jewish city, a retirement settlement and even a spa town. But while the living conditions in Theresienstadt were certainly 'better' than in the death camps in Poland, they were still inhumane.

When Moritz and Else arrived at the start of 1944, the camp was already overcrowded. The rooms in the barracks held between 30 and 60 people, with approximately 2 square metres for each inmate. There was scarcely any privacy. Six people shared each three-tiered bunk bed, and what few personal possessions they owned had to be stored at the foot end. A nail hammered into the bedstead served to hang up their clothes. The rooms were dirty and gloomy, the few windows partially blacked out. Bedbugs and fleas made spending time in the bedrooms unbearable. When the weather and the guards allowed it, the prisoners spent every free minute outside. But free time was rare. Moritz and Else have been working as much as they can: it entitles them to a larger food ration.

In the spring of 1944, the illusory hope that there would be an improvement in their living conditions gained currency. The cold, damp barracks were slowly getting warmer, and news circulated that there would be a 'beautification of the city'. The Nazis wanted to prove to the world that the reports of crimes against the Jews were false. In order to put on a convincing demonstration of this, Theresienstadt was staged as a model camp. Both the place and the prisoners were exploited for this perfidious performance. The Nazis needed to deceive a delegation from the International Red Cross that was coming to Theresienstadt to see things for themselves. In the lead-up, the camp worked flat out. The SS left nothing to chance in its efforts to transform Theresienstadt into somewhere that seemed fit for human beings.

The prisoners were made to sweep all the roads and barracks and paint over the crumbling plaster on the façades. In the 'city park', which the prisoners were not actually allowed to set foot in, they sowed seeds and even planted rose bushes. In a few of the sleeping quarters – those earmarked for the inspection – the three-tiered bunk beds made of raw, crooked wooden slats were replaced with neatly carpentered two-tiered bunks. Chairs and tables, which were otherwise not available and normally wouldn't have fit between the narrow rows of beds anyway, were quickly acquired and set up in the bedrooms. Other lodgings were completely emptied to make way for a library. A sporting field with a paddling pool was constructed, and the workshops were refurbished. To prevent the camp from seeming overcrowded during the inspection, thousands of inmates were deported to Auschwitz shortly beforehand.

On 23 June 1944, the stage was set. It was a balmy summer's day – perfect for the SS's production. The Red Cross committee consisted of two representatives from Denmark and one from Switzerland. The inspection followed a plan worked out in minute detail. The campaign was a success. Although it is hard to imagine

that the delegation didn't realise that this was all just a performance, they returned to their countries with favourable reports,
noting a certain 'psychological pressure' among the prisoners.

The first act in this piece of theatre was to be followed by
another: straight after the visit by the International Red Cross – the
makeshift 'beautification' had not yet faded – SS Sturmbannführer
Hans Günther directed the renowned Jewish actor and filmmaker
Kurt Gerron to produce a film. Gerron, who had previously shot
films with Heinz Rühmann and Marlene Dietrich, was himself a
prisoner in Theresienstadt at the time and was now supposed to
make a film about 'everyday life' in Theresienstadt. Artisans at
work, sumptuously laden tables, a football match in front of a
sell-out crowd, concerts and lectures – all this was orchestrated
for the camera. The film had not yet been fully edited when almost
everyone involved, including Kurt Gerron himself, was deported
to the gas chambers at Auschwitz.

The duplicity and cynicism of this 'city beautification' is made
evident by the wave of deportations that began just a few weeks
later. In the autumn of 1944, trains headed for the killing centres
in Poland left Theresienstadt nearly every day. Among the 20,000
people deported were many of Moritz and Else Gans's friends and
acquaintances, who had come with them from the Netherlands.
Moritz and Else were lucky. Disabled and decorated veterans of
the First World War were still 'barred' from further transport.
Moritz could prove that he was both, and so, for the time being,
he and his wife remained in Theresienstadt. By now, though, any
last faint illusion that everything could end well must have evap-
orated. The optimists in the camp fell silent, and the atmosphere
grew increasingly oppressive.

The number of prisoners in Theresienstadt had more than halved through the deportations, so the work assignments in the ghetto were reorganised. The minimum working age was lowered to 10 years old, and the amount of work required was raised to 70 hours per week. Else now reported for cleaning duties at the Sudeten Barracks – the SS duty station – at 5am every day. Moritz stayed in the cobbler's workshop, through which he could put aside a few extra food rations. This is how they survived the winter.

Now, in the spring of 1945, new rumours are circulating in Theresienstadt every day, giving hope and remobilising strength. Berlin has already been liberated, Hitler might already be dead, and the Red Army can't be far off. In her work in the duty station, Else watches the SS men burning records. But along with this good news, the last days of the war bring new trains to Theresienstadt every day. British and American troops have already arrived in the concentration camps in Buchenwald, Dachau and Bergen-Belsen. Shortly before they got there, the SS guards loaded thousands of inmates onto trains to Theresienstadt, which has still not been freed by the start of May 1945. Horrifying news arrives in the camps along with the transports. Moritz describes this period in his diary:

> 5am, I come back from work and see livestock wagons: the latest transport. Else and I stand at the window. 'An awful sight.' [. . .] Everyone is crying. The German SS stand impassively by without carrying anything; the Czech gendarmes remain uninvolved. (20 April 1945)

As soon as a transport has been unloaded, the next one rolls in. The platform runs right up to the Hamburg Barracks, where Moritz is housed. Over the past year, he has usually only jotted a few words in his little diary; now, he puts his impressions down in writing nearly every day. He wants to bear witness to, and probably also come to terms with, what is happening in front of his eyes:

> Prison uniforms on open goods wagons, young Burschen and Mädchen, as they say in Saxony, all half dead, 14 days on the road, only 400 grams of bread, we give them everything we have, but they can't eat – no saliva. 12 dead girls in one wagon, 70 dead in total, over 100 died while being unloaded; the ghetto is working feverishly, but where can the people go? Everyone is lice-infested, neglected. Barely unloaded and five new transports. Dreadful. Men that look like animals, wave upon wave, famished, half dead; then more female workers, in the same condition. We spot people we know: girls sent from here to Poland in October tell us horrific things. Birkenau: all children under 14 and those unfit to work gassed, 20,000 a day, you can't believe it, but these are reliable, serious people, we know them. (21 April 1945)

Accommodating the ever-increasing number of camp inmates is getting more and more difficult. Food rations are reduced again: 650 grams of bread for four days. Moritz gets a bad eye infection. Else is severely affected, both physically and mentally. She is feeble, can't sleep and is anxious about how much longer she will be able to hold on. But they keep working so that they have enough bread.

> Tuesday, 1 May: Theo's birthday. Else is here at 7 o'clock already. We just squeeze hands. We have tears in our eyes.

Wednesday, 2 May; Thursday, 3 May; Friday, 4 May: Every day brings new excitement and rumours.

Pencil sketch of Moritz Gans by Hans Polak (1884–1969), Theresienstadt, 5 May 1945

On 5 May 1945, the SS, which has been increasingly overwhelmed by the chaotic conditions, hands responsibility for Theresienstadt over to the International Red Cross. Not far from the camp, scattered German units are fighting the advancing Red Army. The war is not yet over here. The Jewish Council of Elders – the body tasked by the Nazis with administration of the ghetto – asks the remaining prisoners to keep calm, maintain order and not leave the camp yet: the place that has imprisoned them for so long might now offer some protection. For the whole long day of 8 May, while the rest of the world is celebrating the surrender, there is still gunfire outside the camp gates. Two prisoners are killed by grenades. A few others are injured. Nerves in the camp are running immeasurably high: after persevering and surviving for so long, will they now fall victim to the war's last battle?

Towards evening, the gunfire starts to let up. As darkness falls, a woman's voice suddenly cries out in Yiddish: 'A roite fun!' – a red flag. A short time later, as the clatter of tank treads grows louder and louder, weak throats fill the camp with vigorous cheering. At around 9:30pm, the Red Army reaches Theresienstadt.

Nevertheless, the withdrawal of the SS and liberation by the Red Army does not spell the end of danger to life and limb for the remaining prisoners. Typhus, typhoid fever and other illnesses break out and the Red Cross doctors, who now have access to the camp, are powerless to help. After its liberation, more than 1,500 more people will die in Theresienstadt, including many doctors and nurses who came to prevent the spread of the epidemic.

The Free Republic of Schwarzenberg

Manfred and his driver decide to make more enquiries in nearby Zwickau about what awaits them in the Ore Mountains. But either no one can or no one wants to give them clear information. On the way to Aue, they arrive at another roadblock: the end of the American Zone. All that can be seen on the other side is German soldiers and civilians. Manfred asks the American guard if he knows where the Russians are. 'Haven't seen any Russians yet, there are none in ERZGEBIRGE. If you got to your destination and back it will sure be as good as any Commando job you have done. Wish you good luck.' Without knowing what lies ahead, Manfred and Bob pick up speed.

> AUE. The city is still German. German police on the street. Thousands of German soldiers. I stand up in the Jeep. They crowd around us; it is impossible to get through. 'Are you coming or are the Russians?' 'Can you take us prisoner?' After a while we manage to get moving again. The town is undamaged, it is unlooted. This is the last glimpse of Germany as it was. The Germans are well-dressed and well-fed. They look bitter and hard. Hysterical women are crying. A sinister people. Push on. I feel scared. Pick up a wounded German soldier and his girlfriend who are going in our direction. That will afford some protection.

The jeep has neither roof nor doors, just a small windshield to protect the field of vision. Manfred is still standing up in the front right of the car; Bob is sitting at the steering wheel. The German soldier and his girlfriend squash onto the small back seat next to their modest baggage and the provisions for Theresienstadt. The banged-up jeep battles its way over hilly roads high into the Ore Mountains. For months, Manfred has been travelling almost exclusively through ruins; the villages and towns that they are now passing through show not a trace of combat.

I still fear mines. There are lots of roadblocks and perfectly good anti-tank guns covering them. But amongst all this I am over-awed by the beauty of the countryside around us. Steep mountains covered with tall and slim fir trees. The road winds itself through them. Occasional fast running rivulets. The German girl is small, round faced, dark haired and wears the traditional dress of the Erzgebirge; white blouse, gaily stitched with flowers, black frock, stitched again with all colours, square cloth braces. She looks terribly sweet and talks that very sweet local dialect. 'This is a beautiful country.' I say. [. . .] She gives us some sandwiches – natural honey! They leave us in SCHWARZENBERG.

What Manfred did not know back then is that a small area in the Ore Mountains remained 'unliberated', even after the German capitulation, for another 42 days. Neither the Red Army from the east nor the US Army from the west marched in. To this day, it is speculated that this was a simple geographical misunderstanding – the Russians and Americans came to their agreement about using the Mulde River as a demarcation line without realising that three rivers with this name flow through the region – but there are countless other theories about why the Ore Mountains avoided the Allies' attention. In any case, the inhabitants of the 21 towns in the district of Schwarzenberg are confused. Thousands of Wehrmacht soldiers on their way back from the east take advantage of the situation and congregate in the Ore Mountains. Even after the capitulation, entire German units muster there in rank and file for morning roll call. The unoccupied areas are gripped by uncertainty. The old order has lost power, but no new force has taken its place in this 'no-man's land'. Action committees are convened to try to create structures – some of them, especially in the town of Schwarzenberg, are full of old communists. Their existence is not to last long, but these circumstances offer plenty of room for speculation and utopian ideas, and many myths and legends have evolved out of these post-war weeks in the Ore Mountains. The myth of the 'Free Republic of Schwarzenberg' has also been shaped by Stefan Heym. His 1984 novel *Schwarzenberg* stages a thought experiment in which the unoccupied region is taken over by an autonomous socialist government. In reality, the novelist was not far away from the Ore Mountains back then: he witnessed the end of the war as a US Army soldier in Bad Nauheim. His life story is astonishingly similar to that of Manfred Gans.

Heym, born in Chemnitz in 1913 as Helmut Flieg, grew up in Germany as the son of Jewish parents. He left his home immediately after Hitler came to power, going first to Prague and then to the USA. There he became a member of the US Army and part of the Ritchie Boys, a unit of German-speaking immigrants in the USA who were used for special missions in the war against Germany. Just like for Three Troop, the Ritchie Boys' most important weapon was language. On 6 June 1944, Stefan Heym landed on a beach in Normandy just a few kilometres west of Manfred, but he mostly supported the advance into Germany with his typewriter, not his gun. While Manfred was convincing the Wehrmacht to surrender face to face, Stefan Heym conveyed his messages to the enemy in writing. As sergeant in a unit for 'psychological warfare', he was the editor of *Frontpost*, a US Army newspaper that aimed to have an ideological influence over the German armed forces, thus weakening their resistance. At the same time as Manfred was on his own mission east to look for his parents, Stefan Heym was travelling tirelessly through the ruined country, looking for functioning printing presses that could put to paper what he and the Allies wanted to tell the Germans. When returning from Braunschweig to his unit in Bad Nauheim, he decided to take a detour through the Russian Zone to see his old hometown, Chemnitz. In his 1988 autobiographical narrative *Nachruf*, he remembers:

> Was homesickness at play? No, Chemnitz was never that nice, and what happened to him there, and to his father and mother, had not made him any more sympathetic to the place; but he did want to see the city again. Chemnitz was like a chapter in his life that was still missing its end.

Despite all these parallels, Manfred and Stefan Heym probably never met. It is equally unlikely that Stefan Heym was familiar with Manfred Gans's official travel report, but the scenes in Heym's *Schwarzenberg* strongly resemble Manfred's experiences in the area, which he recorded in his travel report:

> Now we are on top of the ERZGEBIRGE. Driving into a small village of 2,000 inhabitants. There are 15,000 German soldiers concentrated here. They still have their weapons. I pull up. Hundreds immediately collect around us. 'What is this!,' I enquire. 'Sammelstelle Infantry Divisions.' [. . .] There are thousands

of German civilians with them who try to evacuate Czechoslovakia before the revenge reaches them. [. . .] Again I am besieged by crying women. 'We cannot live under the Russians, they rob us.' I answer, 'Your soldiers have done the same in Poland, Russia, and Holland.' Gosh! My heart stands still, what am I saying amongst 15,000 armed German soldiers? But they let it pass. There are good and bad amongst every people. At last somebody comments on my excellent German. I tell them not to panic. Drive on slowly. Gosh! if I could loot here. [. . .] I could make myself rich for the rest of my life just on gold and jewels which every person, I am sure, is hiding somewhere. Everywhere, hard-faced German girls are lying around with their soldiers. Many wear trousers. There is a lot of charm and sex appeal about them. They look the sportive type. It's their eyes that are unnatural. Later I was to learn that the German women just haven't got a mind of their own anymore. When they open their mouths one might as well put on a record of Goebbels propaganda.

They continue: up hill and down dale. The brakes are completely shot now. Luckily, there's not much going on in the streets, but Manfred and Bob still only escape a collision by a hair's breadth. Then the car gets a flat tyre, too. They are able to get hold of a new wheel at short notice, but the engine starts running hot again uphill. The jeep needs to hold out for at least another 150 kilometres; finding a replacement vehicle so far from the British and US forces would be out of the question.

Between all the people passing by, Manfred suddenly spots British uniforms by the side of the road: former prisoners of war trying to get to the west.

Are they happy to see us!! We dish out fags. Tell them to make for KARLSBAD. Now we meet small groups every five minutes. Our fags go rapidly. Some look as if they had a rough time, others look very well. It depended on the camp they were in. Some have been on the road since Christmas. The Germans made them march 40 miles a day. They are full of horror tales, but all repeat, 'But you want to see what they do to the Jews.' 'No punishment too hard for the Germans.'

Manfred and his driver eventually reach the main road heading eastward to Prague. Past Komotau, they finally meet the Russian Army. Convoys of tanks, trucks and all kinds of military vehicles roll towards them. Manfred can barely stay in his seat. Every time the Russians signal to him, he asks Bob to stop the jeep for a quick conversation to clarify things. A Russian military policewoman – one of nearly a million women who served in the Red Army during the Second World War – asks in broken English whether he is American and what he's doing here. The conversation falters. Manfred tries in German. She is thrilled and, also speaking in German, replies, 'British Officer speaks German; like me spreche alle Sprachen.' She gives Manfred an exuberant embrace and waves him through: another 40 kilometres to Theresienstadt.

In Teplitz-Schönau, Manfred asks for directions one last time and learns that Theresienstadt was freed by Russian troops just a few days earlier. Unlike in many concentration camps, there had apparently been no mass executions in the final hours. On 14 May 1945, after three days in the jeep, Manfred arrives at his destination.

At last THERESIENSTADT. Civilians show the way to the Ghetto. I always thought I would die with excitement at this moment but I am pretty cool now, only that queer feeling in the pit of the stomach which I get before a parachute jump. Check guards outside the 'camp' [. . .] I tell them what I want. First they jump to attention, then a Captain comes he says, 'If your parents are in the part where there is typhus, promise me that you'll come back.'

CHAPTER SEVEN

THERESIENSTADT

It is already evening when Manfred enters the Theresienstadt ghetto. A massive star-shaped fortification surrounds the camp. The jeep drives slowly through a barrier. Manfred is standing in the passenger seat, leaning on the windshield.

I realize what a moment this is. It might have been a scene in Lordship Gdn, London, on Saturday afternoon. There are people – Jews – in the thousands everywhere. They look undernourished, overworked, but fairly well dressed. Western Europe's Jews, every face seems to be familiar. They are all ages, but every eye reflects senility and tiredness. What a grim sight!! I cannot even force myself to smile at them. Everybody crowds around. Drive on carefully. Some are too weak to get out of the way quickly. This is the way we drove into the liberated towns of France, Belgium and Holland.

The crowds were the same, but what a different atmosphere! [. . .]

All eyes are on us, but they are too stunned to utter a sound. I can only look at them grimly.

The Theresienstadt camp was not built from scratch; it was an old garrison town. The wings of the mostly three-storeyed buildings in this well-planned city stretch out over hundreds of metres along the grid of streets. Manfred asks Bob to pull up in front of the registration office. Bob waits outside while Manfred enters the building. A young woman is still working. Surprised but friendly, she greets the officer in broken English. Manfred tells her the names of his parents and asks her to look them up in the records. The young woman opens various folders. She freezes, and then gets extremely animated. 'They are really still here, are you lucky!! I must go with you myself, though I nearly die with excitement.'

The camp had originally been designed for about 7,000 people. When Manfred reaches Theresienstadt, there are almost 30,000. Manfred, his driver and the woman from the registration office make their way to the Hamburg Barracks, one of the largest complexes in the camp, which mostly houses Jews from the Netherlands. Accommodation and social life in Theresienstadt were largely divided along national lines, and, since Manfred's parents had been deported from the Netherlands, they assume that Moritz and Else would be in the Hamburg Barracks.

We can hardly get through the crowds now. Where do all these people live? What a terrible overcrowding! Light inside some of the windows reveal beds and tables made out of raw wood. Everywhere there are double, triple bunks. Stop! This is the house. The girl enquires. My parents are having supper on the balcony. I send her forward and wait in the corridor. Human beings everywhere! No privacy here! I am getting slightly excited.

Damn it I have jumped out of aeroplanes, I am not going to let this get me down! That does the trick. Still looking grim with my arms crossed over my chest.

Manfred sends the woman ahead to prepare his parents – he doesn't want them to get too great a shock at seeing him suddenly standing in front of them. Perhaps they won't even recognise him? It has been almost six years since they last saw each other.

Manfred waits a minute or two. There are still large crowds of people around him. He looks over at the stairs the woman disappeared up, into his parents' lodgings. Slowly, he follows her. When he is finally standing at their doorway, he catches sight of them. Manfred pauses, struggling to keep his composure. Moritz and Else cannot hold back their emotions.

I suddenly find myself in their arms. They are both crying wildly, it nearly sounds like the crying of despair. I look at father and in spite of having prepared myself for a lot I have to bite my teeth together not to show my shock. He is hardly recognizable! Completely starved and wrecked. My first regular thoughts after a few minutes are, 'What a grim show.' The next our old Commando watch word, 'Don't panic!' I lead them to the balcony and force them to sit down. They still can't utter a word for crying. Some of their friends, fine people, come to calm them down. Now at last I manage a smile. People rapidly collect in the yard beneath the balcony. They all shout 'Congratulations' and 'Mazal tov' to my parents. Now they are cheering. That rectifies my parents. Father is completely calmed down now – one look into his eyes convinces me that his spirit is completely unbroken. He still is the old realistic idealist he always has been. During the next few hours I have a lot of reasons to admire him. Mother looks aged, but tanned and fit. There is still a lot of youth about her.

News from the Hamburg Barracks quickly spreads around the camp. Many want to share in this joyful moment, even if only with a handshake. A crowd forms in front of the building. A few young women bring flowers. Manfred gives a short impromptu speech. He talks about the Allied war effort, D-Day, the heavy fighting in France, the invasion of Walcheren, the endless winter in the Netherlands and the huge crowds of people travelling down all the roads in Germany, searching for a future. More than anything, his audience wants to know more about the situation in Palestine, which at the time was still under British administration. Many of the inmates hope to find refuge there.

Meanwhile, their descriptions give Manfred his first details of life in the ghetto, which he has only been able to guess at until now.

They tell me of the horrors they have gone through. Is there any need to repeat them here, after all the accounts in the press? Still it strikes me much harder now.

Although Nazi propaganda had consistently portrayed Theresienstadt euphemistically as a 'Jewish settlement', and even though historians still debate to this day whether it was more a ghetto or a concentration camp, it was certainly a key component of the Nazi's campaign of extermination against the Jewish population. Of the roughly 140,000 people who arrived in Theresienstadt between 1941 and 1945, including around 15,000 children, nearly 90,000 were deported further east to a Nazi death camp. Almost all of them were murdered there immediately upon arrival. Over 33,000 people were killed or died as a result of disease and malnutrition while in Theresienstadt. Fewer than two in ten of the camp's 'residents' survived the Holocaust.

> I've just got to get back to normal thinking. I remember we haven't eaten or drunk anything since 7 o'clock that morning. It is now 8 o'clock at night. I fetch the driver up. Mother is all for him, he is a nice London kid, and full of understanding. We have lots of Ersatz [substitute] coffee. Somebody produces Matzot saved up from Pesach! Mother has Kartoffel Knodle. Amongst talk about their past, our relatives, the world at large, we all feel very happy now.

Late that evening, Manfred goes to see Commandant Kuzmin, the Russian who has been managing the camp for the last few days. He is in a meeting with his staff. They have their hands full trying to stop people dying in the camp after the liberation. Medical assistance from the Red Army only arrived in Theresienstadt the day before. Six hospitals have been set up and are now housing over 4,000 patients. Commandant Kuzmin stipulates that the ghetto inmates should receive the same food rations as his soldiers.

Manfred gives him his letter. Kuzmin has already heard about Manfred's arrival and immediately asks whether he has found his parents. When Manfred tells him about the reunion, he detects a faint smile on the commandant's face, but then he is back to business again. He wants to know whether Manfred has been immunised. Tuberculosis and typhus are out of control in the camp. Manfred can show his soldier's book, where details of all his vaccinations are thoroughly recorded. After being liberated, some of the survivors of Theresienstadt, especially those from surrounding regions, had already tried to leave. As a result, typhus has now spread to some of the surrounding villages, so the Russians are placing the camp under strict quarantine. No one is to be allowed in or out. But the commandant says he will 'close both eyes' and grants Manfred a few hours with his parents.

It is dark now, and the sky is full of stars. Manfred's driver Bob decides to spend the night outside with the car. He is still being besieged by people asking after relatives in England. Manfred and Bob cannot accommodate the many requests but promise to take letters with them if they have them by the next morning. Finally, things start to quiet down.

Now Manfred wants to spend some time alone with his parents. Their bunkmates clear the room for Moritz, Else and Manfred. They stay up talking for half the night. When Manfred hands over the packages he got from the US colonel in Oberlungwitz that morning, his parents can hardly believe their eyes.

> Father nearly cries when I gave him several hundred English cigarettes. That will make him a millionaire here, he says. [. . .] We open that huge box of American 10 to 1 rations. Even to me they look a treasure.

Manfred's parents go to bed at 3am. Before falling asleep, Moritz writes a few lines in his diary.

At half past six in the evening on the balcony, Manfred; at three in the morning, in my bed. All the anguish of the last years are forgotten: the boys are alive, and I can tell from what comes out of Manfred's mouth and the letters that they are still the same. I lie awake in bed until 6am. I still can't believe that we are united with everyone. The good that Manfred has brought us and the bad that we have lived through – it all seems like a dream. (14 May 1945)

Manfred also retires. But he doesn't get a wink of sleep.

What a misery! I could cry all night. As father said, 'We can never pay them back.' What hope is there? I try to reason it out. The young ones will pull through no doubt. Most of them, except Germans, want to go back into their respective country. The rest hope for Palestine. Will they be let in by the English? Will a nationalistic policy that cares for the maintenance of the healthy only not spoil the last hopes of these poor individuals? My parents too want to go to Palestine, but to Holland for recuperating first. For many there is that tremendous question whether the liberated countries will let state-less Jews back into their territory. And above it all, there hovers for me only (not for them) that great question, 'Will it be peace with Russia?'

At 6am, Manfred is back on his feet and treating himself to a clean shave. A quick look outside tells him Bob is up too, and Else has already conjured up breakfast from the American supply package. But Manfred has no appetite and, instead, meets with the leader of the Dutch Jews in Theresienstadt. Before the war, Professor Eduard Meijers was one of the leading lawyers in the Netherlands and a highly respected man in the country. In Theresienstadt, he is a member of the Council of Elders. He too has been ravaged by the previous months, but his mind is unaffected. He asks Manfred to pocket a letter containing an urgent appeal to the Dutch royal family – similar to what he had already written two days earlier in a letter to a professor he is friends with:

> The longer we remain here, the more perilous our situation becomes. In view of the danger of infection, we Dutch must leave here as quickly as possible, if one does not want the last remnant of Dutch Jews to perish here. Give this letter to all the authorities to read, including Princess Juliana! [. . .] We feel we have been abandoned by everyone and everything.
>
> In great haste – Eduard Meijers (12 May 1945)

Manfred must make haste now too. As the morning draws on, more and more people come to him with letters. Manfred asks a young woman to sort them for him. Some people try to convince Manfred to let them go with him; one man even offers him the directorship of three factories he owned before the war: 'if you can make your way here, you can do anything'. Manfred must refuse all these propositions. He has his doubts about whether the Russians will even let him out. The Russian camp commandant had made it extremely clear that he would make an exception for him, but only for a few hours, and that Manfred would not be allowed to take anyone with him. So the two British soldiers must depart at lightning speed – just as Manfred is accustomed to from many missions on the front.

> At 10 o'clock I tell the driver secretly to pull up in front of the house. Letters are still pouring in, some people beg frantically to get favours. In a small room I say goodbye to my parents, away from the crowds, then I rush downstairs jump on the jeep and drive to the gate at top speed. The guard looks doubtful, I say, 'engelsk Offizier' so he shakes hands and opens the gate.
>
> Standing in the Jeep we chase once along the outside of the camp to show my parents that we got out all right, then we are off.

Manfred has had to leave his parents behind, and not just because of the Russians' conditions; it would be too dangerous to drive back with civilians in the jeep, and the strain of the journey might be too much for his weakened parents. Although they may still be trapped in the camp, Manfred leaves with the happy feeling that his parents are now inwardly liberated.

In fact, his father writes the following in his diary:

> Else and I stay back and study Karl's, Theo's and Recha's letters and reminisce. All day long, friends come to congratulate us and hear about it. The entire ghetto is sharing in our happiness. (15 May 1945)

While leaving Theresienstadt behind and on the journey back to his unit, Manfred continues to feel the excitement of the reunion reverberate within him. The return trip is exhausting, though. The driving conditions are poor and their battered jeep still does not have functioning brakes – every time they want to stop, they must let the car slow down and then jump out and use their own bodyweight. Added to this, they constantly come across British and American soldiers heading west from POW camps. A US soldier collapses in front of them, the last remnants of a uniform covering his emaciated body. Manfred left all the cigarettes and food in the camp and doesn't have anything more to hand out. One by one, he picks up returnees who seem particularly exhausted and takes them to the nearest Allied headquarters. It takes Manfred and Bob three days to get back to their unit in Goes.

A Report Goes Around the World

On the night of his return, Manfred puts his impressions from the trip down on paper. He writes both to digest his experiences and to record his many observations from those chaotic post-war days. This is not only for his family and friends; he is also obliged to report on his week-long excursion to the commanding general who gave him permission to go. Manfred asks a sergeant orderly in the office at Goes HQ if he will make some copies, and he sits down at the typewriter and starts typing right there and then. Soon after finishing, his companion comments that this report is an important historical document and asks whether he can keep a copy. Manfred agrees and also quickly sends a copy to his brother Theo in England. Theo sends a telegram to their

brother Karl in Israel: 'FRED WITH PARENTS HEALTHY
BUT AGED'. In another telegram, he writes: 'FRED REPORT
SPIRITS UNBROKEN'.

The travel report spreads at lightning speed, reaching family
and friends all over the world. A few weeks later, Manfred
starts receiving letters of congratulations from every direction:
'everyone must be terrificly proud of you and so am I. I just
could not with the best of my imagination imagine your parents
faces.' – 'Dear Freddy, that was really the best bit off news I have
received since the war started.' – 'Lets hope they soon get out
of there and everybody else!' Anita also responds to Manfred as
soon as she receives his report:

> Freddie, thanks for sending me the report of your trip
> to T. I am so happy your parents are well. I wish them
> lots of luck that they may live in all comforts soon
> again. I'm just puzzled how they ever got there. Do
> give them my very best regards. Your description is
> very good and I almost felt as if I had been with you
> all the time. It must have been a terrific experience.
> You know, dear, I often wonder, how will you ever
> be able to settle down to normal life again after all
> these exciting years. Don't you think it will feel quite
> strange to be completely independent again and to
> have to worry how to pay for your meal and lodgings.
> Of course, I know, it is every soldier's dream to be
> discharged after a certain length of time, yet, it will be
> very hard. (3 July 1945)

Letter from Manfred to his brother Theo after his return from
Theresienstadt, 19 May 1945

Despite all these congratulations, Moritz and Else are neither safe nor free. They are still stuck in Theresienstadt, where disease continues to run rampant. Manfred's mission is not yet over. But he has a plan.

The Return

Queen Wilhelmina returns to her home in the Netherlands in March 1945. She has spent the last five years in exile, first in

166

London and then Canada. Now, she is about to cross the border from Belgium and wants her return to be very conspicuous. When she reaches the village of Eede, she climbs out of her armoured car and strides ceremoniously across the border, which has been marked for the occasion by a thick trail of flour on the ground. On either side of her stand Allied soldiers saluting and peasants cheering her on. Back in the Netherlands, she and her daughter Juliana initially reside at the Anneville Estate in the south-west of the Netherlands, near Breda – not far from Goes, where Manfred is stationed with his unit. He knows the royals are there through an acquaintance who is an aide-de-camp of the royal family.

On 20 May 1945, one day after returning from Theresienstadt, Manfred drives up to the Anneville Estate in his jeep with the letter Professor Meijers gave him in hand. He discovers that it is not the queen but her daughter who is responsible for the repatriation of Dutch Jews. Manfred is asked to wait for Princess Juliana in the manor's reception hall. She has guests and is short of time, but comes out briefly to hear this British officer's request. Manfred relays the situation in the ghetto in a few words before handing over the letter. The princess asks him to make an appointment with her aide in the next few days to discuss how the Netherland's Jews can be retrieved from Theresienstadt. But the meeting never happens: Manfred is relocated from Goes to Germany. Now a few hundred kilometres further east, he can no longer personally see to the return of the Dutch Jews and his parents. But even without his support, everything is immediately set in motion, and transport for Jews from the Netherlands who are stuck in Theresienstadt is organised.

On 21 June 1945, Moritz and Else Gans finally get on a plane in Pilsen. When they board, they don't yet know where it will take them, and even less what they can expect when they get there. The main thing is that they are leaving the camp behind them! In his diary, Moritz Gans notes:

> 16:00 – Embark, take off, magnificent weather, marvellous flight. Else is airsick. I enjoy it. 19:30 – We land. Where are we? It is Eindhoven! Joy, transport, reception at Philips factory. Back at last, marvellous! (21 June 1945)

But will they be able to stay? Even in Theresienstadt, the Dutch Jews had distinguished themselves from German Jews who had been deported from the Netherlands, hoping that it would improve their status among the inmates. In Theresienstadt, it didn't help. But now that they are free, it isn't clear whether the once German, now stateless Jews will be allowed to stay in the Netherlands. One day after their return, Moritz writes:

> Medical examination, loudspeaker, Else nervous. The stateless are supposed to be taken back to Germany. The Dutch keep leaving; we remain. (23 June 1945)

> I am trying everything to have us released into Eindhoven. L. Jacoby comes – he has a house for us. Wednesday 5 o'clock. I have the papers, our bags are already downstairs. Else, Ludwig and I cross the threshold: after 26 months and two days, free people again. In our first private quarters. Johan Vestersstraat 46. Sleeping in freedom again for the first time, and in a bed. (24 June 1945)

It is practically a miracle that Moritz and Else Gans and their three sons, Karl, Manfred and Theo, have survived the Nazi policy of extermination. But where are the parents' many siblings; where are their nieces, nephews and cousins? A brisk exchange of letters begins. Everyone is searching feverishly for clues and signs of life. The news that Moritz and Else are safe gives them courage in these uncertain times. Moritz's brother Isidor and his wife Hilde write to them from the USA:

> My dears,
>
> It's impossible to tell you how happy we are. To know you are well; it is so much easier for us knowing that at least you, my dears, have been saved. We are all anxious and so unhappy about all the news, some of which is so terrible, but unfortunately, we have not been in a position to do anything for you all until now. [. . .] Unfortunately, we have had no news of Paula and Meta, of Ernst and Suse, but not of the children. Abraham and Helene, Berta and Bennie and where are all the others? Dear Moritz, I am sure that you will spare no effort in finding out. And our poor father, where might he be now? I believe he is no longer alive, but does anyone at least know where he was? (30 June 1945)

As more and more information, reports and images of the extent of the extermination of the Jews become public, their happiness about their own fate is increasingly tinged with sorrow and horror. Moritz and Else write to Else's sister, Henny, in Palestine about both their good fortune and the family's losses:

> The fact that large numbers of us have survived this hell in good health means we already belong to the 'chosen

ones'. When we were in a really bad way – when I felt at the end of my physical strength; when Möken [Moritz] was so exhausted he looked like a beggar – it was only the thought of our children that lifted us up again. It was all worth it. Voilà Manfred, our striker on the left! – It was the best thing we'd ever experienced. Three days after the end of the war, the boy was standing in front of us. It's impossible to describe. [. . .] Since that day, we have been humans again. All at once, the gates of the ghetto opened up before us. [. . .] Sadly, Moritz's mishpokhe has been taken: Meta and her entire family, Paula and her husband, Berta's eldest son Philipp and his family (wife and child) – all victims in Poland. Berta's youngest son Alfred starved to death in Bergen-Belsen. His wife and young daughter returned. [. . .] Ernst's six-year-old son was caught alone. Poland. (12 July 1945)

Around 30 members of the extended Gans family were murdered during the Holocaust. Sixty-four Jews who were either born or at some time lived in Borken were killed. Three-quarters of the Jews who were living in the Netherlands at the start of the war were murdered in concentration camps. Only around 5,000 returned. In no other Western European country occupied by Germany was the percentage of Jewish victims so high.

Chapter Eight

From Freddy to Manfred Again

Manfred has barely been back from his trip to Theresienstadt for a week when more bad news reaches him at his base in Goes. The 41 Commando has been summoned to Germany. As if that wasn't enough, he tells Anita,

> Now you sit down please. – Have you done it? Get hold of your chair firmly – right so.
>
> Where do you think 41 commando is stationed now? – You have guessed it (you are always so dammed quick) Borken in Westfalen. Out of all places! You realize that it has absolutely nothing at all to do with me. We have come here to take over some very definite duties and . . . well here we are. – In the meantime people have recognised me and it has spread like wildfire. Oh by the way the first person who recognised me was a girl that used to be regarded as one of the local beauties (married now, complete with Sprössling [offspring]). I never knew that I was then such a well known person and believe you me I neither then indulged in Rassenschande nor do I now indulge in fraternisation. (1 June 1945)

It seems to be a coincidence that, of the hundreds of places he could have been sent, Manfred ends up in Borken. It actually makes things quite difficult for him, as people are continually asking him to use his position to help them.

He has to go to his parents' house regularly now, which has become the headquarters of the AMG. One day, his old biology teacher, Mr Dahmen, shows up there out of the blue. Manfred recognises him immediately and, after a moment, Mr Dahmen also realises who is standing opposite him in a British soldier's uniform. Friendly and interested, he asks how Manfred has fared. Manfred relates his deployment to the front, his trip to Theresienstadt and the reunion with his parents. Then he quickly excuses himself, as he is expected elsewhere. A few weeks later, Mr Dahmen shows up again – this time he has sought out Manfred intentionally. Other former teachers have already asked Manfred to help with their denazification: if he officially confirmed that they had not been Nazis, it would protect them from criminal prosecution. Now Mr Dahmen is also hoping that Manfred will put in a good word for him. After all, he argues, he hadn't 'snitched' on Manfred and his brothers when they had so vehemently disagreed with him in their racial science lessons; if he had reported it, they, and possibly also their father, would have surely landed in prison. Manfred really did wish some of his old teachers well, like his form teacher Mr Tinnefeld. But not Mr Dahmen. In an interview with Hans-Jörg Modlmayr in Borken in 1999, he remembers his retort:

Mr Dahmen, we don't need to talk about the more than 20 million fallen Russians; we don't need to talk about the six million dead Jews; we don't need to talk about the 250,000 Allied soldiers killed in action in Europe; we only need to talk about the 200 boys from Borken that died: they are your responsibility! You are responsible for them! For if someone who is a doctor of biology talks such nonsense about racial science, it's your responsibility. There is no way that I will support you in getting a denazification. We're done!

Manfred cannot evade his teachers and other former functionaries in the city, but he initially avoids contact with people his own age. Sometime later, however, a young woman Manfred is still familiar with from his youth is employed by the Military Government. He is unable to avoid her there and writes to Anita:

we got involved in a long long discussion, and I was most interested to get the views of some of my old Pennäler [schoolboy] crowd. From her and two other chaps whom I met later and who have just returned I gathered that amazing impression, that they look at me foremost as one of their old crowd, nobody thinks it funny to see me in British uniform, and they find it most odd that I should feel a very great resentment about the time I spend together with them. – Then I went to see the Bürgermeister. He had just got in the new plan for rebuilding Borken. It will take 20 years time. He proudly displayed the plan and showed me the exact details of a huge synagogue they have included. He was most surprised when I assured him that none of us will come back. He couldn't understand it, and still people won't grasp it that even their local Jews have died a miserable death in the gaschambers. (21 December 1945)

The Kreis Resident Officer of the Military Government, Town Major Cyril Montague Dobbs, learns of Manfred's personal relationship to Borken and his special knowledge of the town, and asks him to join the Military Government in Borken for the longer term. Manfred declines the offer. If he still hoped during his early encounters in his hometown that the Germans would soon face up to their crimes, he is now increasingly exasperated by their ignorance. He writes to Anita:

Don't think for a minute the Germans are still docile! Talking now to all the people I know I notice that though the men have learned their lesson partly, the women have learned nothing at all. Filled up to the brim with Nazi and Germanistic propaganda. Selfishness just isn't the word. They are just horrible. Fortunately they hardly matter anymore. If we keep our peace with Russia Germany will never rise again, if we don't – well that could be the greatest catastrophe ever anyhow.

Needless to say that I am getting a bit of dirty looks on the street – not that I care. One day it might be a bullet though, never mind. (1 June 1945)

Reunion in Freedom

Back in the Netherlands, Moritz and Else use their network to find a room with a family in Eindhoven. A few days after their arrival, Manfred travels from Borken to visit them in freedom. He brings two 'German chickens' with him to be slaughtered for the Sabbath. After arriving at the address and parking his jeep, he goes to the house, only to find it shuttered. He looks around, but there is no one to be seen. After a while, he hears a voice call out joyfully, 'He's here!' It is his mother, who spotted the British jeep a mile off as she was walking down the street.

They serve up a sumptuous feast. For the first time in years, Moritz and Else are dining at a table that has been set with knives and forks, eating from plates and drinking from glasses. Moritz turned 60 just a few days before, but stresses that now he is free, he is getting younger with every passing day. Manfred is astonished at how much his parents have already recovered since their reunion in Theresienstadt. The weekend flies by. There is still so much to tell each other.

Manfred sets off again early on Sunday morning, but not to return to his unit in Borken just yet. His route takes him a good 200 kilometres north. He is embarking on another search: this time, he hopes to find his Oma Bertha, Else's mother. She had been in hiding with her daughter and son-in-law back in Marssum, in the province of Friesland, until just before Moritz and Else were betrayed and deported. With his grandmother's last known address in his pocket, Manfred travels the length of the Netherlands. The weather is superb, and the roads are in better condition than those on the other side of the Rhine. Only once, shortly before reaching his goal, must Manfred cross a badly damaged, shaky bridge. After a good three hours, he reaches Leeuwarden, the provincial capital of Friesland. On the country road leading to Marssum, he stops and asks a woman for directions. He hands her the note with the address on it, and she tells him how to get there. 'I assume you've come to look for "Oma"?' she adds with a smile.

Manfred and his brothers have adored their warm-hearted, witty Oma since they were children and, before the war, often spent vacations with her in Völksen. The last time Manfred saw her was before his parents sent him to England in 1938.

The British jeep crawls up the driveway of a relatively simple farmstead. Manfred climbs out and asks whether this is number 345, the home of the De Jong family. Before the farmer's wife can reply, he sees his little Oma rushing towards him with long strides. She seems to have momentarily forgotten her 84 years. Manfred is still considering how he should greet his Oma when she flings her arms around his neck and covers his cheek with kisses. The farmer and a farmhand emerge from a barn to witness this happy reunion. Once the excitement has died down, Oma Bertha leads her grandson into the house, sits him in a chair and picks her knitting needles back up. He is to tell her everything and not miss a single detail. Mrs De Jong serves up a celebratory supper, and Manfred returns the favour with several packs of cigarettes. Oma Bertha, whom the De Jong family hid for over three years, says they have more than earned these riches. The farmer's wife is still both relieved and puzzled at why the Germans never came to get her. 'Such an old bag'll die soon enough, no one wants her anymore,' Oma states plainly. She is now known by everyone in Marssum as 'Oma', just as she used to be in Völksen.

A few weeks later, Moritz and Else go to collect Bertha. But in the summer of 1945, they still don't know where they will end up.

After some back and forth, they are given Dutch citizenship, finally putting identity documents in their hands after years without them. They don't want to stay in the Netherlands for long, though. They still aren't sure whether they will emigrate to Palestine or England, but one thing is certain: they will not return to Borken.

Manfred doesn't have many nice things to report from Borken. When he sees how its citizens cheer returning soldiers, he interprets it not as an expression of their relief at being reunited, but as evidence of a militarism that has not yet been defeated. In a letter to Anita, he writes:

> The other part of recent happenings is what is going on in this town. The sons of the fatherland are now returning en masse, and here under our eyes we have to watch the most fantastic spectacle ever: a beaten army that has brought nothing but misery to its own people, getting the most fantastic welcome ever. Every time a truckload of them passes through, the whole population particularly the girls turn out and everybody cheers and jubilates. Never will we recieve such a welcome in England and that is all for the good too, because I dislike the deification of soldiers.
>
> Several deputations from the town with petitions have been recieved by me, and eventually turned down. I have told them outright that unless the so-called intellectuals would start enlightening their people on such ideas as Antisemitism, warguilt, etc. I was not going to consider any of their petitions, though I was former citizen of the town. (18 June 1945)

In one of his letters, Manfred includes a photo that shows him posing in front of his family home in Borken, looking serious but utterly confident of victory.

Manfred in front of the Military Government HQ in Borken – his family home, June 1945

The photo stirs up memories for Anita:

> My dear, you can hardly imagine how surprised I was when I received your last letter with the pictures of the house. For a minute, I wished I could be there with you and walk through the fields behind the house. Then sit in your room and chat, after a swell dinner in the dinningroom around the round table and then just sit back on the couch in the spacious livingroom and listen to music. But, as I said that was only for a minute, I was back here in New York immediately, being very thankful and happy. I am glad you too had thought of me when

you walked through the house for the first time, we did have a good time these 5 days I spent with your family. That is all long ago and just a very pleasant memory, one of the very few that we have of that country. But, it has really nothing to do with that country, if you could transplant the house and all that goes with it over here or to England how much freer and happier our thoughts would be. (30 July 1945)

Anita wonders if Manfred's parents know about their exchange, to which Manfred replies that he told them during their first reunion in Theresienstadt. Anita's mother has also found out that they are writing to each other again; she is clearly not thrilled about it, but doesn't try to stop her daughter again.

Yes, life does play all kinds of queer tricks on people. More and more I become convinced of the injustice and unfairness of it all. I don't believe Freddy, we are the only ones who feel that way; the war has taught us all a big lesson. We have seen with our very own eyes that in many cases the best have not been spared any fate, whereas. . . but why say it. Let us just hope and do not give up hope for a better and just world to live in. We probably will not live to see it, but, I am convinced, once the world or rather universe, as it becomes smaller by the years, will be an accomplished Utopia. Mind you, I am not saying now, but much later. And here again, we can say that it isn't fair that we have to suffer for something we will never be able to enjoy. That is the vicious circle of life, I suppose. And that is where you need faith. (30 July 1945)

In September 1945, Moritz and Else return to Zandvoort, where they had lived for a while straight after fleeing Germany and still have some friends. Here, they slowly start to establish the rhythm of their own lives again. Moritz writes to Else's sister, Henny, in Palestine:

> My dears, we are well, and we moved into our own little house again eight days ago. This is a special privilege, for there are no apartments to be had here. But the local municipal council catered for us splendidly and gave us a little house that had been confiscated from its Nazi owner. We are very happy about it, because now we can at least have Manfred under our own roof. We have also been lucky with our furniture. Friends were able to save around 90 per cent of it. Only linen, clothes and Mesumen [money] are gone. But we are making do. The main thing is we can cook again, and Else has been sleeping on her mattress again for the past eight days. I'm not yet, but the bed from the national manufacturer is still better than the last two-and-a-half years of sleeping on a wooden box with a straw sack. (14 September 1945)

To bring in some income, the pair soon rent out the guest room in their little house near the beach. During this period, Manfred is able to visit his parents every second Sunday and watches them slowly find their way back into their middle-class life of the pre-war years. He describes it to Anita:

> Gosh kid, if you havn't had a home for a long time it's damned funny to come to a place that has all the assets of home (parents, great comfort, the pieces of furniture you know etc) and still you can't get used to the idea that this is your home. Mother is still as careful about one's health, well being etc as she used to be in peace time, quite ridiculous if one looks at the things one has gone through, but still its damned nice that somebody does make a fuss. (19 February 1946)

On one of Manfred's visits, Moritz asks his son to go with him to Leeuwarden. Now that they have somewhere to live and Oma is back with them again, he wants to find the valuables that he had entrusted to the policeman Jan Willem Smouter before the war. Moritz has heard that Smouter had spent the final years of the war living like a lord and had been acting increasingly strangely; in the spring, he had gone to ground. He has now resurfaced and is working in Drachten, not far from Leeuwarden, where Moritz and Manfred meet him.

When they confront him, Smouter tells them he gave the box with their valuables in it to Moritz's nephew Alfred. Moritz is perplexed. Is Smouter really trying to fool him into believing that he, an experienced policeman, had thought the valuables would be safer with a Jew in hiding? He is made even more suspicious by the fact that it is Moritz's nephew Alfred whom Smouter names: as Smouter well knows, Alfred was killed in a concentration camp so is no longer able to confirm or deny it. But Alfred had never mentioned Smouter entrusting him with the box when he was with them for a few weeks in Bergen-Belsen. Before Moritz can give vent to his rage, Manfred weighs in on the conversation. His years in the armed forces have taught him how to assert himself calmly but firmly – and his British officer's uniform lends him additional authority. He warns Smouter that this is his last chance to come out with the truth and reminds him that this box held all that remained of his father's fortune after the Germans had taken everything else away from him. But Smouter fends them off. Moritz and Manfred notify the police. Although it goes to trial and Smouter is eventually convicted, Moritz and Else only get some of their money back.

Interrogations

Manfred leaves his hometown of Borken after five weeks. He has been ordered to go deeper into the Ruhr to Recklinghausen, where the British are establishing No. 4 Civilian Internment Camp. Before the end of the war, the Western Allies had decided to detain potential war criminals and high-ranking Nazis while they were on the march and carried lists of active and staunch members of the Nazi Party and SS on their advance into Germany. By the time Manfred arrives in Recklinghausen, there are already several thousand people detained there. He describes it to Anita:

> We got part of the ex guards of Buchenwald, Belsen and various other notorious cases, but apart from these straight forward cases (I don't see why we aren't allowed

to shoot them) everybody in that camp (exception one good looking slightly mad, B.D.M. girl who is in for espionage) assures you that they have never been Nazis at all. You probably are very interested in 'what they are like'. Well, that's easy, they aren't even interesting. Starting with the lowest grade: the concentration camp staffs, they are just professional criminals highly cranked, there isn't even one who is normal. As our [regimental sergeant major] (he is a fantastically fine and experienced old man) remarked 'when these fellows have been beheaded one will have to tell them that they are dead otherwise they won't know.' High party officials: mostly overambitious men to whom every mean was right to further their own careers. They ought to be punished most, because they are the least naturally 'cranked'. SS and Gestapo: the for ever crawling & obedient type, fanatism I haven't discovered yet amongst them (I suppose the fanatics went into uniform and fought) slightly 'als Kind zu heiß gebadet' [dropped on the head as a baby] (you see what I mean?). (14 July 1945)

Manfred is one of around 20 officers tasked with the interrogations. During this period, he lives in quite luxurious quarters in one of the villas that is still standing, which has been confiscated by the British Army. But he doesn't get to enjoy much of the luxury; he spends the long days in a small, uncomfortable interrogation room in the internment camp. Manfred and the investigation team stoically plough through one case after another. New suspects are brought into the camp every day. Some of the inquiries are wrapped up quickly; some prisoners are set free again after a short time; others are interrogated over and over again for months. When asked about someone else, many of the internees have an awful lot to say; when asked about their own role during the war years, though, they tend to fall silent. Manfred shares his frustration with Anita:

> And here there is not one person (exception the girl mentioned above) who has the guts to stand up and say: 'Here I am, my ideals are Nazi and I shan't move an inch from them.' No, they all whimper when we interrogate them, nobody has ever been more than a simple P.G. [Nazi party member], everybody has done everything to use his position to avert the worst crimes and so on and so forth. (14 July 1945)

What Manfred is describing in Recklinghausen matches the observations of many others in the Allied forces who encountered remarkable detachment in the individuals they were investigating. Stefan Heym said similar things about (re-)engaging with Germans, and Saul Padover, an intelligence officer in the US Army who grew up in Vienna, reported on it extensively. Padover travelled through Germany conducting hundreds of interviews and began drawing up a psychological profile of the German (post-war) population. He came upon feelings of shame, but rarely those of guilt. He seldom sensed sympathy with the victims nor discerned outrage over the atrocities; instead, what he had to listen to was self-pity aplenty and continual relativisations: Hitler had cruelly deceived the Germans; he had promised victory and lots of holidays; the only guilty parties were the Führer and his close followers; they themselves were not personally responsible. Spending time among such people seems to rattle Manfred, and he writes to Anita:

> Are you surprised kid, dass ich hier langsam über-schnappe [that I am slowly cracking up here], with exactly the men at my feet who once were our greatest and seemingly most secure oppressors. (14 July 1945)

Since Theresienstadt, Manfred has asked himself over and over again how the Germans should be dealt with. Sometimes he just wants revenge, then he collects himself and realises that it would bring him neither satisfaction nor relief. In other moments, he asks himself whether everyone isn't partially to blame in one way or another, himself included. If everyone in Germany, and Jews and governments abroad, had been able to look beyond their own circumstances and their own interests back in 1933, if they had come together and been firm in their opposition, might it have been possible to prevent the entire catastrophe that had engulfed the world? He has a lot of questions, but no answers.

Manfred feels like a stranger in the country where he was born and grew up and increasingly yearns for the end of his military service. Every week, there are new announcements from London about if and when soldiers who enlisted for the war can go back to civilian life. Anita also hopes that Manfred will be able to leave Germany soon.

> How did you spend the holidays? Was there a Synagogue around, or don't you believe in going? [. . .] And, how are things with you? Gee, I'm afraid to ask, but I shall

venture it: 'Did you get to England yet?'. I better not ask anymore, but do tell me whatever has been going on with you, and why in the world aren't you getting a discharge? (10 September 1945)

For Rosh Hashanah, Manfred planned to drive to a receiving camp for displaced persons near Diepholz, with the intention of organising an evening for the Jews stranded there with the Jewish chaplain. But he found that the group had already been transferred to Sweden, so he spent the holiday alone, similar to the year before, when he had spent Rosh Hashanah in the Dunkirk sewer system, and yet also entirely different.

Prospects of a speedy return to England soon fade. The government in London keeps promising that demobilisation will be expedited, but older soldiers who have already completed vocational training are first in line – the plan is for them to return to their jobs quickly and jump-start industry in England. There is also a shortage of officers in the ranks of the Military Government. It might take another whole year until Manfred's time comes – provided another war does not break out in the meantime. So Manfred puts all his plans for civilian life to one side again and explores the best way to spend the rest of his time in the military. He has interviews with various detachments and takes on a wide variety of assignments: he completes training as a mathematics teacher for the armed forces in Osnabrück; in Harz, he is tasked with exploring options for setting up a mountain infantry unit; and, for a few happy weeks, he is seconded to train for a sports competition as a middle-distance runner – all he has to do during the day is run and, for this, he gets plenty of good food and massages. Finally, he is tasked with an investigation by the Office of Public Opinion during which he conducts interviews with the German civilian population.

Then, in the autumn of 1945, Manfred finds out that the 41 Commando is being sent to Hong Kong. He does not want to go there under any circumstances. Once upon a time, the commanders of the British Armed Forced had rejected this German refugee; now his knowledge of German is invaluable, and he manages to avoid being sent to Asia. Eventually, Manfred is assigned to the Control Commission for Germany (British Element). They send him into the northern Ruhrgebiet, to Gladbeck.

Reconstruction

Like so much else, Gladbeck has also been decimated. Sixty thousand people are living among the ruins. Together with just two other colleagues, Manfred is charged with reconstructing civilian life here. He is responsible for public health and utilities, education, road transport and information control. British Army experts provide advice, but the organisation on the ground rests entirely with Manfred and his colleagues. The range of tasks is immense and, to keep up with them, the Military Government engages a considerable number of Germans. Manfred complains that he thinks many of the people employed by his fellow officers seem to have been close to the Nazis. Apparently, the British are primarily concerned with ensuring that the administrative bodies and other establishments run smoothly and efficiently. Whether someone was part of the Nazi regime is becoming less and less important. Manfred operates differently. When one of his administrative staff whose sympathies he doubts starts exercising more and more power, he dismisses him summarily even though he knows he will be difficult to replace.

As assistant commander of the Military Government in Gladbeck, Manfred is now also tasked with overseeing denazification of the civilian population. He describes the proceedings to Anita:

> Yesterday was the first meeting of our newly set up denazification committee. It consists of the Oberbürgermeister, the three party leaders and two Beamte known for their anti Nazi behaviour. As long as any one of them vetos any man in an official position the man is fired. Now the leaders of the Comunist and SPD are terrific guys with ten times as much idea about democracy than a dozen British officers, still I was surprised to see how many cases the did NOT veto. I had thought they'd clear the place out. Still the final decision was with us so we cleared out 6 (of 12 cases considered) reduced the salary and status of 2 and left the other 4 in office. That was a clean sweep to my liking. (3 January 1946)

Wherever Manfred goes, he now carries a list of wanted people with him. It is both a blessing and a curse that he speaks the language of the defeated and can conduct the interrogations for many of the difficult cases himself. These interviews are often a great strain on him and some of the interactions shake Manfred's faith in humanity, which he has not yet lost entirely. He tells Anita:

It is quite unbelievable the amount of people who from sheer maliciousness completely ruined their neighbours. In my opinion the tragedy of fascism were not so much the big crimes like the War and the K.Zs [concentration camps] but the meaness, the small mindedness, the utter maliciousness and corruptness and materialistic egoism and selfishness and brutality, which the ordinary little citizen (of every country!!!!) displayed once the fetters of ordinary laws were removed. [. . .] Where you spit (apart from the 10% of really good people) you find people who used the general chaos to betray or swindle not only other people, no even their best friends and closest relatives. (15 December 1945)

During his time in Gladbeck, Manfred has a room in a house to himself and a maid comes in now and then to look after the fire for him. His main leisure activities are reading books and writing letters. Now that his unit has left, and his friends along with it, and since the last few months have been spent constantly pursuing a new task in a new place, he has barely anyone familiar around him. But he finds a new friendship in Gladbeck. Isidor Kahn, the only Jew left in the town, comes to visit him every day. Like Manfred's father, Moritz, he had run a successful textile business before the war. He survived the war years in hiding. He is happy to have met Manfred and, on their very first meeting, asks Manfred if he can procure a tallit and tefillin for him. Manfred immediately passes the request on to the Wislickis in Manchester, with whom he is still in regular contact, and is soon able to present his Jewish friend with the requested prayer shawl and phylacteries. Mr Kahn shows his thanks with a sumptuous Sabbath meal. Manfred describes their gatherings to Anita:

> I wished you could join us in one of our Schabbath after-noon parties for when he starts telling stories of the years he lived 'underground' [. . .] he can be too funny for words. On the other hand he has lost practically all his family and that has broken him nearly completely. His hatred knows no limits. I am sure he was the only person in this town welcoming the ration cuts. At the moment he lives from the parcels he gets from his relatives through me. (12 March 1946)

Two years later, when Moritz Gans gets his textile business back, he hands it over to Isidor Kahn at his son's request.

Manfred has been promoted again and is now a captain. He still has a lot to do, but then he has always enjoyed being challenged. Having just settled into his role as assistant commander of the Military Government in Gladbeck, Manfred receives shattering news: first, the Ministry of War in London has decided that it will no longer employ officers of German origin in the Military Government. He must give up his position in Gladbeck. Then, during a short visit to England, he learns that the places that had been reserved for young returning soldiers at English universities would no longer be available. To help him process all this news and uncertainty, he starts writing to Anita more and more often:

> I quite often get depressed too, and with the speed I am living at that is only a very natural physical reaction.

After all one experiences so many thrills and exaltations that that ones mind just has to swing round to some other moods occasionally. As long as one doesn't become a bother to other people in those moods I don't think it makes any difference.

Gosh kid I'd give anything to see you in an evening gown! Perhaps I'll have that pleasure one of these days. (30 March 1946)

Rapprochement

Manfred and Anita have written each other hundreds of pages of letters over the last seven years, but they have not seen each other even once. Since their romance in the summer of 1938, both their lives have changed drastically. They have become adults and have survived flight, persecution and war. Anita finds herself questioning whether their connection will also survive the war:

I am so glad that you are well, now that the worst is over. [. . .] I am just wondering if we will be able to understand each other; do you think we will manage? or maybe better leave it at writing. It's the safest. (5 June 1945)

Manfred also feels that real life might not live up to their letters, but thinks that it's high time they saw each other again anyway.

I have got the feeling we are idealizing each other too much and probably a lot of that would be dispelled on meeting face to face. Well we'll see . . . (28 July 1945)

In one of her letters, Anita suggests that, with everything he has experienced, Manfred should write a book. But Manfred is sceptical and wants to look forwards rather than back:

> As regards writing books well you know my answer there. I don't think my experiences so far in my life have been very singular or unique yet. About 'settling down to normal life' well though I may run parallel with ordinary careers occasionally I have no intentions on settling down into a secure 'Spiesser Dasein' [petty bourgeois existence] again. (14 July 1945)

Back in her 'normal life', Anita has found a fulfilling job with CBS radio in New York. She works for Arthur Godfrey, one of the most famous radio and TV presenters of the 1940s. On the weekends, she increasingly spends her time enjoying New York's clubs and bars. She is 22, sociable and attractive. Anita has many admirers and is constantly writing to Manfred about her latest marriage proposal. She declines them all. Manfred is still somewhat peeved, though, perhaps even a little jealous, and complains that she shouldn't brag about her men to him.

> My dear Anita, your letter of the 30th is just about the limit. Or that means that one sentence in it where you tell me about that friend of yours who just proposed etc etc [. . .] you must be a very attractive person, only I hope you know what you are doing refusing all these chances. (14 November 1945)

He later – somewhat flippantly – suggests that, with her great collection of marriage proposals, she must know all the techniques and can eventually advise him on the matter. At the same time, Manfred tells her bluntly about the beautiful French maid in Gladbeck, a close friend in the Netherlands or a girlfriend he met in Wales before the war. The two of them may have already guessed that their real happiness lies on the other side of the Atlantic, but in their letters they feel their way carefully forwards. Anita writes:

> No, I'm not bragging that I'm being proposed to you every hour on the hour – in the contrary, if that would be the case, it would be a fine mess. The whole thing is just too funny to describe, so let's skip it. Sometimes, I feel that you got the wrong idea of me. I suppose as much as a person can be natural and herself in a letter, it's never the same as talking. Maybe the recipient often interprets things differently than what they are supposed to mean, and I believe I probably do the same with your letters. You once said so rightly, 'it's time we meet' and that'll probably take a lot of the sugar coating off; ha ha, but what a surprise if there is none. (5 December 1945)

In her letters, Anita has repeatedly expressed concern that the war might have changed Manfred. She hardly wrote about it during wartime, but, now that the war is over, she either cannot or does not want to hide her fears any longer.

> From all your letters I have noticed that you became so terribly self-centered that no other person but yourself matters very much, and, if so, it is only for your own pleasure or comfort. I did not want to say this but you kind of asked for it. I suppose the war has a lot to do with it, naturally your own life becomes the most important, but

still there is no excuse. I have not realised this because your letters are not personal, as you say. I think they are tops, by the way, just like I would want you to write, there are no tricks on my part, even enjoy your sarcasm. No dear, what I said, I read between the lines. I know war is bloody and makes a person tough but still there is kindness and understanding in this world. As you said, 'All your dreams have come true', that's fine but don't be too conceited because of that. Sometimes I have the feeling as if you think you are superman. You've always been very sure of yourself and I think that is very important and necess. in life to get ahead. There is little greatness in a person though who has been successful and let this go to his head. I'm not saying this is the case with you, but it might come to it. Maybe that's British, if you want to call it that, but for us here in America and in general life simplicity and understanding for others and also the underdog is the finest character trait in any person. Without it, in my eyes, a person will never amount to much. Our last president was great because he was understanding, tolerant and simple. – Freddie, remember when you flunked the matric the first time and your Dad said: 'I'm glad, it will be a lesson for you'? Jeepers, I don't want to preach, far from it, besides I probably became a bit too involved! (5 June 1945)

Life in Limbo

Manfred has now been serving in the British military for over five years. He has risked his life and climbed up the officer ranks.

But he is still not British. While Poles, Frenchmen and Danes who fought for Britain in the No. 10 (Inter-Allied) Commando have been naturalised without great difficulty, the Home Secretary, Herbert Morrison, remains sceptical about the German refugees in the armed forces. Several MPs in the House of Commons raised the matter during the war, but Morrison would not yield, indicating that his ministry couldn't process the additional applications anyway – there were more important things to be done in wartime. After the end of the war, the Skipper, Bryan Hilton-Jones, now safely back in England after his time in German imprisonment, writes a letter to the ministry in strong support of his men. Before deployment, the USA had offered the prospect of citizenship to all refugees who joined the army, and Anita can't understand why Britain is hesitating:

> Did you became a British citizen yet? I too always get terribly furious whenever I hear of cases like yours, but you better not let me get started on that. (3 July 1945)

Manfred declares that he stopped wanting to become British a long time ago: he still hasn't really taken to the country. Later letters show that he doesn't believe the British owe him any particular moral obligation, either. 'Surely they realise as much as we do that we didn't fight [. . .] for them.' But with the end of his military service approaching and the need to organise his civilian life, he still wants to try to get a British passport.

> By Gum if they put me before a board or such like thing they are going to hear a thing or two!!! As far as travelling is concerned naturalization will probably make a

great difference, but as far as the jobs etc are concerned I don't think it will change anything as the British Authorities have acquired that nasty habit of asking for 'British born'!

Please press both thumbs that the present recruiting drive in England will be a great success, because on that will depend the future speed of our demobilization. (30 March 1946)

Finally, in the summer of 1946, new ways of becoming naturalised open up and Manfred immediately fills in all the necessary forms.

Manfred often spends what little free time he has making enquiries into the whereabouts of friends' relatives or delivering packages for them. His good position means that many avenues are open to him, but, every now and then, when it all gets too much, he doesn't find it too hard to say no to these favours – at least to close friends. When it comes to requests from Moritz and Else's friends, though, it's a different matter: he would do anything for his parents.

Meanwhile, Moritz is trying to get compensation for the property expropriated from him in his homeland. Manfred travels to Borken several times on his behalf to get documents about the house. There, he is helped by Hermann Finke, the very same municipal employee who was able to help some of the Jews of Borken flee Germany before the war, including Manfred's parents, and protected others from deportation to the east. At the same time, Moritz and Else are making plans to follow their eldest son Karl to Palestine. They want to set off as soon as their application for restitution has been processed. Manfred writes to Anita:

The Old Man (that's my father) is worrying his head off, that now where we could do with some of his money (which we all have refused to accept ever since we left school) he hasn't got any left for the 'kick-off'. Particularly his one ambition in life – even still when he left the K.Z., and didn't know yet what had happened to his fortune – was to set up Karl in a farm of his own and than live there with him. Not that that is worrying us in the least, aber er macht sich schwere Vorwürfe [but he is kicking himself], and I feel quite sorry for him. (30 August 1946)

Gans Again

Before Manfred's commando days draw to a close, his language skills are once again required and he is deployed to the frontlines one more time. In the spring of 1946, the 'front' is the interrogation of German war criminals. After being forced to give up his position in the Military Government in Gladbeck, Manfred goes to the No. 5 Civilian Internment Camp in Staumühle, near Paderborn. It is the second-largest internment camp in the British occupation zone, and, one year after the end of the war, nearly 10,000 potential war criminals are still sitting in jail here waiting for their trial. Among them are many prominent cases. Manfred encounters guards from Auschwitz and other influential Nazis, like Alfried Krupp von Bohlen und Halbach ('a nasty bit'), who put tens of thousands of slave labourers to work in his armament factory.

The new job is turning out to be most thrilling. Very negative in a way, interesting not in the sense that a study of medicine is interesting, but in the way one reads a good thriller. Some of the stories that come out in the course of these interrogations are too fantastic for words and reveal a deep view of the amazing human character. (26 May 1946)

The interrogations go from nine in the morning till six at night. No German employees are allowed in the review and interrogation department, so, after the interviews have finished, Manfred must do all the related paperwork himself. Without the support of a handful of other German-speaking Jews in their ranks, Manfred is sure that they would never get anywhere near managing the workload. The working days are long and challenging: 'I feel as if I have done two parachute jumps for these interrogations require a great amount of concentration,' he tells Anita.

Camp Staumühle is well outside the city, and the old inn that Manfred is staying in is further from the camp again. He is well provided for, but finds little diversion in the solitude. He describes moments of excitement blurring into an 'ocean of boredom' in one letter to Anita, and it becomes increasingly easy to read signs of fatigue and loneliness between the lines of Manfred's letters. But an end is in sight.

Love ain't rationed, but you know in the army everything is rationed (even bread as we sometimes find out to our discomfort) and when it comes to Love, well there just ain't no telling of the shortage of the thing. (What exactly does all the above mean, can you make it out?) Nevertheless I think I could spare a lot for you. (23 June 1946)

On a Saturday in August 1946, Manfred – who has still been living under the name Frederick Gray – is demobilised. Practically overnight, this officer of the British armed forces, who until recently had his own car and staff, becomes a civilian without a fixed address or source of income.

> Well I better tell you how it all happened. I left Paderborn one lovely day and reported to some Transit Camp near Hamburg. There, our papers were being checked, which took a full day, but one was allowed to go out during this time and I spent the day sailing on the Elbe. [. . .] Next day we sailed from Cuxhaven and got to Hull the following day. Company aboard was rather pleasant, though all the demobs a bit depressed, we tried to celebrate our last night in the army, but got pulled up by the Captain for having girls in our cabin. Food was just terrific on the ship, they really do a lot for demobs, and I suppose this was the last time for a long while that I have been travelling first class. Next evening we got into Hull and from there to York, where we went through the demobbing routine on the following morning. Fitted out with a civvy suit etc I left for Manchester [. . .]
>
> Life here is complicated: to-day I got all my various ration books and coupons, I really don't know yet what is what. (20 August 1946)

Although many of his Three Troop comrades will keep their English names their whole life, Manfred sheds his false identity along with his uniform. At the end of the letter in which he tells Anita his military days are coming to an end, Manfred adds a short, handwritten note: 'It will soon be GANS again.'

Back in England – 'feeling very cheerful and at peace', as he tells Anita – Manfred can finally complete his naturalisation process. Through a fortuitous administrative error, Manfred's case is prioritised, and he must wait only six weeks for an interview instead of the usual nine months. In mid-September 1946, shortly before the Rosh Hashanah holidays, he travels down to London to attend another interview with the British authorities. Unlike back in 1943, this time he knows exactly what to expect. Everything goes well, but the papers are a long time coming.

When he became a soldier in the Pioneer Corps six years earlier, Manfred had sworn his loyalty to King George VI. Despite this, he was not a British subject for the entire length of the war. In June 1947, Manfred will swear almost the exact same oath of allegiance, only this time to finally become a British citizen. In his naturalisation certificate, it states: 'I, Manfred Gans, swear by Almighty God that I will be faithful and bear true allegiance to His Majesty, King George the Sixth, His Heirs and Successors, according to law.'

In a thick folder in the London National Archive, just two pages after Manfred's naturalisation dossier, is the certificate of Maurice Latimer, his comrade from Three Troop, with whom he fought side by side in Normandy and Walcheren.

Anita had already received her long-coveted US citizenship on 9 May 1945, one day after the German capitulation. She proudly had herself photographed in front of the Manhattan skyline on the occasion and sent a copy to Manfred.

Anita in New York, May 1945

Rendezvous

Back in civilian life, Manfred is again staying with Leo and Luise Wislicki in Manchester. He is furiously studying for a university entrance exam, but exactly what will happen next, and where, is completely open.

> Personally I'd have no objections to start off in the U.S., in the long run I don't think I want to tie myself to any country. So far I always made friends easily and one finds

likable people anywhere, so I am not scared to leave here. Settling down here would of-course have some advantages, only it would be rather difficult to find a suitable sort of society to live amongst. I don't know whether you quite get that, you see, the people I have known before the war, were mostly orthodox Jews into whose society I don't quite fit anymore, the people one lived and died with during the war, were great fun whilst it lasted but the few amongst them that were really 'my types' are now scattered into all winds and I am not one for keeping up huge correspondences. Now one really starts all anew again, which to me is great fun. (27 August 1946)

Manfred has made inquiries about going to the USA, but quickly discovered that visas are only available for business or to get married. He decides to try his luck at the consulate anyway, where they ask him if he wants to marry the woman he plans to visit. Manfred replies bluntly that, after eight years without seeing her, it's hardly a question he can answer. He receives a sympathetic smile, but no visa.

At the same time, Manfred finally receives a place at university in Manchester, which he doesn't want to give up. It becomes apparent that Manfred will not be going to the USA, at least not any time soon. But what about Anita?

So there we are I seriously don't see a chance to come over-there, and all I can suggest is that you come over to England. In that event I would be quite willing to contribute 50% of the fares.-----No, I ain't kidding this is a serious suggestion,

after all we have to get down to brass-tacks sometime or
the other. So give it a thought. (12 July 1946)

Now Anita tries her luck. She has a girlfriend who recently
emigrated to England; but she too was only granted an entry permit
so she could get married there. Another friend wants to help Anita
get a business visa for England. This would make things easier. In
Anita's case, though, it's not enough to convince the authorities;
she must also persuade her parents. Her mother does not approve
of her daughter's plans. She barely knows Manfred, after all, and
England is so far away. Manfred writes to her:

> I don't think your parents are far wrong when they
> think you are slightly nuts, for that matter I wouldn't
> be surprised if the two of us finished up 'in the Snake
> pit'. I've never told my parents yet that you are coming
> overhere, though they have a vague idea that I was going
> over to the states sometime. – I don't think that they are
> going to like it much, but that can't be helped and if they
> had been here during the war, there would have been a
> lot of things which they wouldn't have liked either – like
> the rest of my friends who always dissuaded me from
> exactly the course I eventually did take, but after all it's
> my damned life. (2 November 1946)

Manfred and Anita are in agreement: they will ignore their parents'
wishes. It's more complicated when it comes to the hurdles erected
by the authorities, though. Anita's application for a business visa is
rejected. Manfred assures her that he will take care of it, but, as it

happens, he can't straighten it out. The application had apparently been rejected in the British embassy in Washington.

> How are you, lady?, still in the blues? From your letter you sounded a bit reconciled again though. Probably you have realized the sames as I have, that it doesn't matter two much about a few month earlier or later, you'll be disappointed early enough. (14 December 1946)

Though 1946 ticks away without any progress, Manfred and Anita do not give up. At the start of the following year, their hard work finally pays off: Anita receives a temporary visa for Great Britain. The two of them start to make concrete plans for spring, when Manfred has his Easter break, starting with a week in London. He writes to Anita:

> I don't think I feel exactly afraid of your coming over, but there is one thing I felt very uneasy about: if you should be very disappointed when you come here, and all the illusions you might have about me, should be blown away, you would be feeling very awkward indeed on returning and facing your friends and family, most of whom probably know all about this story. (12 January 1947)

Meanwhile, Manfred is studying chemistry in Manchester, and he has not lost any of his determination. He studies and studies. The first university exams are in the middle of March – and shortly after that comes a test of a completely different kind.

[T]his is my last letter to my little dreamgirl, if ever I shall write to you again I shall at least know what I am writing to. May be I'll like the reality better than the dream, may be not . . . I've got an open mind on this. However it was all great fun whilst it lasted and it ought to finish with a really nice letter [. . .]

I just haven't time to think of it all yet, but once the examinations are over that will be quite different and I suppose I shall get the 'jitters' again then [. . .].

Well, Anita, I wish you a lot of luck for the whole of this adventure. Have a good time on the Q.E., they say one easily falls in love on a sea journey, well <u>don't</u>, and I hope the guy whom you meet at the other side will behave himself (that would be a change!).

For the last time kisses 'on account' and meet you in Southampton. (10 March 1947)

Reluctantly, Anita resigns from her job at CBS. Getting several months' holiday or a leave of absence would be unthinkable in this industry or in those times.

In the middle of March 1947, the *Queen Elizabeth* sets sail from Manhattan with Anita Lamm on board. It is her second Atlantic crossing. Before the war, she left Germany headed for New York; now she is returning to Europe to meet a man she last saw as a 14-year-old. Anita is now 23.

During the passage, she writes a letter to her parents:

So far everything has been just swell – the first morning was a bit tough going till I got used to the boat, but now

I don't know anymore that I'm on the ocean. [. . .] The people are friendly and nice but no rich millionaire yet to fall in love with – of course, that's all I would have needed.

[. . .]

Wednesday – 11:30 A.M –

The weather: ideal

I feel: fine

The boat: rocks

I think: of you!

[. . .]

Thursday –

One more day, my darlings, and I'll be in England. [. . .] [W]hat happens from now on I don't know and all I can do is hope and wish that whatever I'll do and decide will be right and good. (25 March 1947)

At 3:30pm on the dot on 28 March 1947, the *Queen Elizabeth* ties up in Southampton. The sun is shining. It is very warm. Anita is standing on deck, her eyes scanning the pier, but she can't find Manfred. She must be patient. The passengers aren't allowed to leave the ship until the entry documents have been processed onshore. This takes hours. While still on board, she receives a wire from Manfred: he is waiting for her in the port.

At 7pm, Anita goes ashore. While waiting for customs to be finished with her baggage, she searches frantically for her friend. She is starting to fear that she might have missed him, which would be quite the catastrophe. Where and how would she find him? She is just in the middle of organising with the guard for her baggage to be kept back for a later train to London when suddenly, out of nowhere, a strange man throws his arms around her. Later, she tells her parents about it:

> Well, after all of my unsuccessful attempts to locate the right person, I was very happy to see that Fred had recognized me first – as I had already started seeing him in almost all kinds of men on the dock. (30 March 1947)

After eight years, Manfred and Anita are standing face to face once more. This first encounter lasts no more than a moment. Anita already has a reservation for the train about to leave for London and must jump aboard; Manfred will follow on a later service. He just has time to slip her the address of their hotel. A few hours later, at midnight, they can finally greet each other in peace in the lobby of the Hotel Imperial in central London. A few days later, Anita writes a reassuring letter to her parents in New York:

> Well – here I am and very happy. Fred is absolutely a dear and not at all as tough and hard as we were all afraid. He is very good to me and we could not possibly get along better. But before you judge me hard for thinking of Manfred this way so fast – you can rest assured and you will not have to worry that I am foolishly deciding things or rushing into anything. We are both very aware of the necessity of getting to know each other much, much more and better. We have talked over these things at home often and I as well as Fred fully realize the dangers we may run into if we became foolish and irrational. So, Darlings, put yourself at ease. (30 March 1947)

Manfred and Anita in Aberdovey, 1947

After just a few weeks, Anita extends her visa and ends up staying nearly half a year. The pair visit Moritz and Else in Holland and travel to many places that Anita knows only from Manfred's letters. They cycle over the dunes of Walcheren, where there are still broken-down tanks, and hike through the hills around Aberdovey, where, in Manfred's words, he was 'reborn'. At the end of May, they are engaged. The Wislickis, who forwarded the letters between Manfred and Anita for all those years, organise a small party for them. In September, Anita must return to the USA. This time, though, the pair say their farewells knowing that they will see each other again.

Getting the marriage visa for the USA is now a simple matter for Manfred. Six months after Anita embarked on her journey back to New York, Manfred boards the Polish passenger ship *Batory* in

Southampton, just a few kilometres from where he had put out to sea four years earlier on a troop carrier headed for Normandy. On 12 July 1948, his ship arrives in the port of Manhattan. Anita is already waiting for him on the pier. Just before departure, he had sent her a quick telegram:

Off, to marry you!

Manfred and Anita at their wedding in New York, July 1948

Ten years after falling in love in Borken, Manfred and Anita have found their way back to each other. They live in Manchester until Manfred has finished his bachelor's degree there and then move to the USA shortly after. Manfred continues his studies at MIT in Boston and then carves out a career as a chemical engineer. The pair have two children, Aviva and Daniel. The family eventually buys a house on the Hudson River, in the shadows of the Manhattan skyline.

Manfred's brother Theo studies agriculture in California and then, like his brother Karl before him, moves to Israel in 1952, part of a wave of emigrants dreaming of 'making the desert bloom'. Moritz and Else follow their sons to the newly established state of Israel not long after. Their former home in Borken is now far away, both on the map and in their minds.

Else and Moritz Gans with their three sons in Israel in the 1950s

CHAPTER NINE

REUNION IN BORKEN

Manfred's career as a chemical engineer takes him all over the world. The family spends a year living in France and half a year in Spain; he spends several months in Japan, and every month he flies to London for business. In his role as an adviser for the United Nations Industrial Development Organization, he is also active in Cuba, China, India and Vietnam. From time to time, his work also takes him to Germany, sometimes even to the Ruhrgebiet, but in all these years, it never occurs to him to make a detour to nearby Borken. He and Anita have built a life for themselves in the United States. Their origins have receded into the background; perhaps partly because they sense that the country they grew up in hasn't yet come far enough that they want to see it again.

It took Germany decades to begin to face up to its history and finally break its silence. Many families only spoke about the war circumspectly, and the Holocaust was often completely edited out. Even into the 1960s, schools in West Germany still only touched on the genocide of the Jews. Events commemorating the end of the war in the young Federal Republic of Germany balanced Germany's crimes against the suffering of German expellees and bomb victims, without considering the root of the evil. Even when the '68ers began to scrutinise the role of their parents' generation, silence was often put before reflection in both the private and political spheres.

At the start of May 1985, Helmut Kohl went to a military cemetery in Bitburg with the US President Ronald Reagan and laid a wreath at a memorial there, surrounded by the graves of soldiers from the Waffen-SS. Three days later, on 8 May, Germany's then-president Richard von Weizsäcker – who himself had fought on the front for six years as a Wehrmacht officer and whose father, as State Secretary at the Foreign Office, had been an important functionary of the Nazi regime – contrasted this with one of the most influential speeches of the post-war period: in 45 minutes, he effected a historical and political change in (West) Germany. As a young lawyer, Weizsäcker had stood by his father's side in front of the Nuremberg War Crimes Tribunal and tried to find words to mitigate his father's guilt. Now, four decades later, he put guilt at the centre of Germany's historical consciousness. On the 40th anniversary of the end of the war, he addressed both houses of the German parliament in Bonn, using words that challenged especially those who had also served as soldiers in the war. His speech on German history made history:

The 8th of May was a day of liberation. It liberated all of us from the inhumanity and tyranny of the National-Socialist regime. Nobody will, because of that liberation, forget the grave suffering that only started for many people on 8 May. But we must not regard the end of the war as the cause of flight, expulsion and deprivation of freedom. The cause goes back to the start of the tyranny that brought about war. We must not separate 8 May 1945 from 30 January 1933. There is truly no reason for us today to participate in victory celebrations. But there is every reason for us to perceive 8 May 1945 as the end of an aberration in German history, an end bearing seeds of hope for a better future.

Within a short time, millions of copies of Weizsäcker's speech had been printed and hundreds of thousands of sound recordings pressed. Weizsäcker's words hardly sound progressive today, but, in 1985, they were met with both agreement and disapproval. Several of Weizsäcker's party colleagues (for example, the CDU parliamentary party leader Alfred Dregger and Bavaria's Minister-President Franz Josef Strauß) criticised his speech and – long before any real coming to terms with the Nazi era had even begun – demanded that a line be drawn under it. Among historians, it triggered a debate about the singularity and comparability of the Nazi crimes. Weizsäcker's speech also inspired many people across the country. In many places, interest in genuinely engaging with the crimes of National Socialism grew – including in Borken.

It is Borken in the 1980s, and Mechtild Oenning (later Mechtild Schöneberg) is investigating the role of the Catholic Church in National Socialism as part of her degree dissertation. Through her research, she becomes aware of her hometown's long since vanished, now almost forgotten, Jewish community. She finds names and researches the addresses of former Jewish inhabitants of Borken who had survived the Holocaust and sends letters out in every direction. Her first answer is dated Christmas Eve, December 1987. It is from Herbert Jonas, Manfred's cousin, who was born in Borken in 1925 and now lives in the USA. He is pleased that someone is finally concerning themselves with the Jewish history of Borken, his hometown, and assures his support in her research. Herbert Jonas forwards the query to Hans-Fried Gans, another cousin, who then sends it on to Manfred. Manfred informs his brothers, Theo and Karl, who in turn tell many other former Borkeners in Israel. Mechtild Oenning and a few allies are soon corresponding with over 20 of Borken's former Jews.

The year 1988 marks the 50th anniversary of Kristallnacht. Mechtild, who in the meantime has been elected as a city councillor, is able to convince the council and Mayor Josef Ehling to invite members of the former Jewish community now living abroad to their former home.

The phone and fax lines between the USA, Israel and the Netherlands run hot. There is intensive discussion among the former Jews of Borken, who have barely had any contact with Germany over the previous decades, but have maintained close contact with each other. Should they accept the invitation? Do they want to? What kind of people and, above all, what attitudes would they encounter in Borken? For some, the road to Borken is still too painful and they decline the invitation, but many more than they dared hope back in Borken say yes.

At first, Manfred – who is now in his sixties – is unsure. After reading Mechtild's dissertation, though, he is convinced: this young generation was obviously facing up to the dark chapters in the history of their city and their country – and, after all, the invitation was also a good opportunity to spend some time with his brothers and sisters-in-law. Manfred, Anita, his brothers Theo and Karl, and 35 others announce their visit. But they have one request: they will accept the invitation to a celebration in the town hall, but they also want to speak in the town's schools. The town and schools are only too happy to accept.

Manfred and Anita meet up with part of their group at the airport. They spend half the night talking across the aisles about their mixed feelings about the journey. One of them, Howard Hahn, jokes anxiously that the invitation could also be a trap to finish off the Borken Jews once and for all.

At 6am, the plane lands in Düsseldorf. Mechtild is waiting at the airport to receive the group. As soon as they meet, Manfred feels reassured that making the trip was a good decision. A town bus is ready for them, and they reach the suburbs of Borken as dawn breaks. Everyone is looking out the windows expectantly at the grey day. As they draw closer to the town, more and more memories float up: a road that has barely changed; a sign pointing to a town that reminds them of a friend in a neighbouring village; then the prison where the town's Jews were locked up on Kristallnacht 50 years ago. Their fatigue vanishes in an instant.

Upon their arrival at the hotel, the guests are greeted with a lavish breakfast and a big hello. Manfred has kept in close contact with some of the people in the group, while others he has not seen since childhood. It is a motley crew: staunch atheists from the Kibbutzim in Israel stand side by side with strict Orthodox Jews from New York. Everything has been thought of. Hans-Fried Gans has brought a carload of kosher food with him from Amsterdam, and his wife, Billy, explains to the wide-eyed kitchen staff what they need to be mindful of in the coming days.

That very afternoon, they begin a long tour of the town's living rooms. Luckily, Manfred and his brothers still have a taste for the rich regional cuisine. They are mostly very warmly welcomed and have lively discussions, but they still feel uneasy in a few conversations. Some comments are painful reminders of old times.

The official programme begins in the evening. It is dark, foggy and cold, similar to that night 50 years ago that they now wish to commemorate. A good 250 people have gathered in a car park in the town centre: the exact spot where the Jewish school and synagogue once stood. The car park is unlit; only a few torches throw a flickering, weak light over the crowd of people, making the photo of the old synagogue projected onto the wall of an apartment block all the more luminous. The parish priest opens the memorial event. Manfred is astounded that the Borkeners know every prayer and every song by heart. Then his brother Theo lays a tallit over his head and takes the microphone. He, too, intones a prayer, this time in Hebrew: 'El Maleh Rachamim' ('God full of compassion'). The Jewish guests then join together to recite the Kaddish, the prayer for the dead. As Manfred will recall in a report entitled '"Meeting the Past and the Present" a Diary of Eight Days in November 1988' written shortly after returning from this trip:

> There, probably for the first time in the 750 year history of this town and the hundreds of years of Jewish life in it, the alleys and the walls were resounding with a Hebrew song. For centuries we had sung Hebrew songs in the Shul and School and in our homes but never out in the open, certainly never within the resonating walls of the inner town.

After the memorial, the travellers sit up for a long time in the hotel to share and digest their impressions of the evening. The night is short, and the very next morning, some of them are standing in the classrooms of Borken's schools.

Manfred visits Borken's vocational school. He tells the students about his childhood and school days in the town, about his time in the military and later deployment. He has barely finished when questions start raining down on him from all sides. The school bell rings, but no one stirs. Finally, the teacher ends the talk, but, before Manfred can leave, a cluster of students and teachers has formed around him, still wanting to ask him questions. Manfred returns to the hotel exhausted but happy.

The days that follow are also intense. The Gans brothers visit their family home, where they are warmly welcomed by the new owners. Manfred and Anita ask them to open up the now locked attic, where they shared their first kiss half a century ago. Together with the other returnees, they visit a memorial plaque recently erected in the centre of Borken to commemorate the Borken synagogue and Jewish community, which bears the inscription: 'WE LET IT HAPPEN. AND THOUGHT NOT OF THE CONSEQUENCES. HAVE WE LEARNED FROM IT?'

Next, they go to the Jewish cemetery where they say another Kaddish: for those who died in Borken during the war but were buried unceremoniously, and for the Borkeners who died in the extermination camps and were denied the dignity of a last resting place. Their place should have been here, among the graves of their ancestors. The return to Borken was worth it if only to pay this tribute, Manfred thinks.

Full of impressions and with several new invitations in their bags, they board a plane back to New York one week later. Once there, Manfred writes:

> We are home in the U.S. again and we are emotionally drained. This was the second most emotionally draining experience of my life, the first being my liberating my own parents from Concentration Camp. But this week we were transposed in time: we abruptly went back to the life which we had left fifty years ago, a life of which we had not too many fond memories and to which we had no desire to ever return – but here we were a gathering of almost ALL the surviving Jewish contempories of fifty years ago now living in Israel, the U.S. or in Holland, lavishly and considerately invited by the descendants or the successors of those whose hostility had driven us out, welcomed by many of our former neighbors and playmates and sought out by a small group of activists who for the sake of honesty and the sake of their children feel compelled to face up to the uglier side of the history of their town and their nation.

Although Anita was not born in Borken, she has many memories associated with it, and the trip leaves strong impressions on her too. She also puts them to paper, in a five-page report she calls 'Kaddish after Fifty Years. One Week in Germany, November 8 – 14, 1988', written in December 1988 after returning from this trip to Borken – her first since 1938:

> We have learned from this entire experience: that the few and the young who reach out to learn from history, and

those who want to understand and face the past, cannot and must not be denied while some of us are still around to help them out of their dilemma. I even found that many of us, maybe not so much I because history treated me kindly, but others, also have not and still are not ready to face up to these years and have shut them away.

I still don't feel comfortable in Germany but if there is a job to do, I'll do it. I don't know how often we will go back again but a small impact was made by us.

Manfred with school students at the Jewish cemetery in Gemen, 1990

Anita would never go back to Borken. Soon after returning from Germany, she fell ill and was diagnosed with cancer. She died in 1991 at the age of 67.

In 1994, the Jewish cemetery in Borken, where Manfred and his companions had been so warmly welcomed, is defiled. Manfred is dismayed at the news. Despite – or perhaps because of – this, he, his brothers and many other former Jewish inhabitants of Borken start returning there nearly every year to talk in schools about their history, the Holocaust and the Jews. As the years go by, they form new friendships in their former hometown.

A Memorial for Aberdovey

Sometime after Manfred's first visit to his former hometown of Borken, the chance for another reunion presents itself. More than 50 years after the formation of their elite unit, the veterans of Three Troop plan to come together again. Their training was intensive and their assignment extraordinary, but, since they were all assigned to different commandos, the Three Troop members lost touch with each other, especially when they were all busy reconstructing their lives as civilians after the war. They live scattered throughout the world: in England, the USA, Australia, Canada and Switzerland. A few of them had also returned to Germany and Austria. Because of this, only a few friendships survived. Only once their – mostly successful – professional careers had drawn to a close did many of the veterans begin to reflect on their time in this unusual unit. Now they want to meet in Aberdovey to inaugurate a memorial commemorating their service and, above all, their 20 fallen Three Troop comrades.

On 15 May 1999, it is all set. Twenty-two former Three Troop commandos, including Manfred, gather in the Welsh seaside town. With Anita no longer alive, Manfred is accompanied by his son, Daniel. They assemble in a small park with a view over the ocean. Several highly decorated, elderly representatives of the British Army have travelled there, and a large number of villagers who still remember the soldiers with the funny accents fill out the ranks. The town choir gets things going with a few Welsh songs, and then the Three Troop veterans form a semicircle around a large stone:

FOR THE MEMBERS OF 3 TROOP 10 (IA) COMMANDO
WHO WERE WARMLY WELCOMED IN ABERDYFI
WHILE TRAINING FOR SPECIAL DUTIES IN BATTLES
1942–1943
TWENTY WERE KILLED IN ACTION

These words, now chiselled in stone, had been wrestled over beforehand in dozens of letters. Some of the veterans were adamant that the troop should finally be called for what it was: a Jewish unit. Others were vehemently opposed to such a description: they had not been chosen for their Jewishness but because they spoke German. A multitude of voices fought for one or the other reading. Manfred positioned himself between these two camps. His Jewish identity was absolutely important to him, even if it was a long time since his faith had been governed by the strict Orthodox way of life he grew up with. But, Manfred thought, it wasn't their Jewish ancestry that should be acknowledged; it was their contribution to victory over National Socialism.

When German resistance to the Nazi regime is spoken of today, many refer to German officers' and generals' failed coup of 20 July 1944, to assassination attempts like that of Georg Elser or to the White Rose information campaign by those including Sophie and Hans Scholl. The fact that the history of Three Troop can also be understood as part of the German resistance, albeit in an entirely different form, has barely been considered until now. In the literature and at memorial sites, Jewish resistance is only seldom mentioned; when it is, then usually only as individual underground activities or uprisings in the camps and ghettos, such as the Warsaw ghetto uprising of 1943. Sometimes, the Jewish Brigade is referenced, a Jewish unit in the British Army that was formed in Palestine and fought against the Germans and Italians, though only shortly before the end of the war. The names of a few of the Ritchie Boys do crop up in lists of memorials to German resistance, including the service of Stefan Heym. But references to the more than 80 Germans and Austrians who fought in the ranks of Three Troop are absent here, too.

In Great Britain, the secret of Three Troop was revealed about a year after the end of the war, and reports on the 'German soldiers' in the ranks of the British armed forces were published. On 24 October 1946, the *Daily Express* quoted Lord Louis Mountbatten, who, not long before, had spoken openly for the first time about the zeal and merit of this unit:

Not a man said no – and none of them let us down.
It is to men like these we must look for the building of a
new Germany.

At the reunion in Aberdovey, Manfred was already suffering from Parkinson's disease and was finding it increasingly difficult to travel. He went to Borken one last time in the year 2000, where he spoke in schools and met up with old friends. In 2010, at the age of 88, Manfred Gans died at home near New York. School students in Borken planted a tree to remember the Gans brothers, the other former Jewish inhabitants and their legacy. Now, at last, the history of the Gans family is once more part of the town of Borken – and Borken is part of their family history.

Epilogue

Our bus slowly rolls down Bocholter Straße. Almost everyone has jumped up from their seats and rushed to the right-hand side of the bus to strain their heads against the glass. From one of the rows, I hear the voice of Manfred's daughter, Aviva: 'There it is! I recognise it.' The bus driver stops and the tour group – 18 descendants of the Gans family – jumps out into the lush front garden. Daniel, Manfred's son, takes some photographs out of his pocket and looks from the old pictures in his hand back up to the house in front of him, recognising more and more features. It looks just as magnificent as before, he exclaims. Luckily, the current owner, a lawyer, has been informed of the family's visit and greets the guests shortly after their arrival with sparkling wine, canapés and open doors – the glasses have barely been emptied when everyone vanishes inside. Soon, the happy faces of Moritz and Else Gans's grandchildren and great-grandchildren are looking out of every window of the (grand)parental home.

Aviva has never been to Borken before, which makes her even happier to be exploring the place she has heard so much about. Above all, she feels that this trip is bringing all the cousins, who live spread out around the world, together in a completely new way. They have all heard stories from their parents and grandparents about their former home, and now they can puzzle the pieces of information and anecdotes together into a complete picture.

After the visit to the 'Gans house', we head to the Hotel Lindenhof, where Manfred, his brothers and the other Jewish guests stayed during those remarkable days when they first returned in 1988. Like back then, the mayor of the town invites the group to a Sabbath celebration, where the next two generations of the Gans family meet the citizens of Borken. There are a lot of lively interactions and long, intense conversations. But, as moving as this visit to Borken may be, it is – like it was for Manfred in 1945 – just a short stop on the journey east.

A week later, we reach Theresienstadt. On this August day, there are not many visitors about, just a few of the town's residents sitting in front of shops and houses. Today, the former ghetto is both a memorial site and a sparsely populated, surreal Czech town called Terezín. The Gans family wanders down the streets, passes the crematorium and stops at the Hamburg Barracks, where Moritz and Else were once housed. For Daniel, Manfred's son, the trip casts this place in a different light:

We knew they had been in Theresienstadt. My father's mother would talk about the recipes they would talk about at the camps. And they told us these stories, but certainly not the horror and the fears that they must have felt. That understanding was not pushed on us as children: that we are the survivors of the Holocaust.

ACKNOWLEDGEMENTS

This book would not have been possible without the help of many people. My thanks go to every one of you, but I would like to name a few here.

Most importantly, I would like to thank the Gans, Ziv and Kaddar families, whom I had the privilege of accompanying on a journey into their family history. They were so open in allowing me to participate in their exploration and made countless materials available to me. I would like to mention Aviva and Daniel in particular, the children of Manfred and Anita Gans. They placed their trust in me and allowed me to dive deep into their parents' archive.

I would also like to express my gratitude to Norbert Fasse for making me aware of Manfred Gans's fascinating life story. It was his inquiry that first put me onto Manfred's case, and our constant exchange helped me to keep following him over the years.

My thanks go to the many historians on whose work I have built. In this context, I am particularly grateful to the working groups 'Jüdisches Leben in Borken und Gemen' and the many similar initiatives across Germany. In Borken, I must make special mention of Mechtild Schöneberg. If she had not got in contact with the Ganses and the many other Jewish families from Borken, it is likely that this biography would never have materialised. In this context, I would also like to thank the many efficient, helpful staff at all the archives, especially Judith Cohen from the USHMM, who has done amazing work with the curation of the Family Gans Collection (The Manfred and Anita Lamm Gans family collection).

I would like to thank the people with whom I had invaluable discussions about the work in various arenas: Malte Berndt, Sandra Holtrup and Brunhilde Valder, who also came on the journey with the family; and Stefanie Wolter, Jasper Stephan and Julius Noack, who helped with transcription and research.

I am grateful to the people who have helped with previous drafts of this biography or contributed to them: Regina Tanne, Christian Staas, Benjamin Leers, Markus Köster, Ralf Haarmann, Jeremias Koschorz, Lucia Schulz, Elias Reichert, Tim Kehl and Christina Ebelt.

The reason that my previous work on this story ever turned into a book was a surprising question from Sebastian Ritscher, who asked whether I would like to write a book on the topic and set it all in motion. I would also like to thank my German publisher, Erik Riemenschneider, for trusting in me and the very fruitful collaboration, and Angela Volknant for the excellent editing of the original German edition. The English edition of this book was made possible by the literary agent Tanja Howarth, publisher Sarah Braybrooke, translator Rachel Stanyon and editor Julia Kellaway. I would like to thank them for their interest in the story and their enormous efforts in realising it.

My thanks also go to Carin, my wife, who gave me the space, even in a turbulent time, to find the peace needed to write and who is there whenever I have any questions or doubts. Thank you to Noah and Paul for all the happiness you give me.

And, last but not least, I would like to thank my father, who transcribed hundreds of pages of letters with so much dedication, deciphering the faintest pencil-written notes and the most illegible handwriting; who commented on the manuscript with so much knowledge and wisdom; and, above all, who passed his interest in stories and history on to me and contributed so significantly to the content of this book.

Image Credits

- United States Holocaust Memorial Museum, Washington, DC, and Daniel Gans and Aviva Gans-Rosenberg: pp. 11, 70, 129, 166, 201, 208, 210
- United States Holocaust Memorial Museum, Washington, DC, and the Manfred Gans Estate: pp. 13, 14, 19
- Leo Baeck Institute, New York: pp. 25, 209
- Aviva Gans-Rosenberg and Daniel Gans: pp. 44, 65, 67, 178
- Giora Kaddar: p. 146
- Imperial War Museum, London: p. 107
- Stadtarchiv Borken, Borken (photographer: Wilhelm Schmitz / photo Schmitz-Dahm): pp 117
- Mechtild Schöneberg, Borken (photographer Maria Wolters-Höyng): pp 219

ANNOTATED BIBLIOGRAPHY

The following list gives an overview of materials essential to the development of the book in addition to the Manfred Gans Collection in the USHMM described in the Author Note on page ix. As well as holding the Manfred Gans Collection, the USHMM has been relied on for many facts and figures about the Holocaust.

Archival Holdings

Imperial War Museum, London
> This contains the *Nachlass* of various Three Troop veterans and interviews the historian Ian Dear conducted with them.

Leo Baeck Institute, New York
> The Lilo Goldenberg Family Collection is held here. It includes countless letters, memories and documents contained in the collection of Manfred Gans's sister-in-law Lilo Goldenberg, born Lilo Lamm.

NIOD Institute for War, Holocaust and Genocide Studies, Amsterdam, and the *Nationaal Archief*, The Hague
> Records documenting the plans for the return of Dutch Jews from Theresienstadt can be found here, along with information on Manfred Gans's role in this process.

The National Archives, London

Among other things, this collection holds the war diaries of Three Troop, No. 10 (Inter-Allied) Commando, No. 41 (Royal Marine) Commando and Manfred Gans's certificates of citizenship and promotion (under the name Frederick Gray).

Stadtarchiv Borken, Borken

This contains a variety of collections from the local press, administration and schools, providing information on the role of the Gans family and the Jewish community in Borken.

Tresoar, Leeuwarden

The records of Smouter's trial are archived here. It also contains clues about Moritz and Else Gans's experiences during their time in the Netherlands.

Villa ten Hompel, Münster

Among other things, this archive contains documents and correspondence about Manfred Gans's visits to Borken in the 1980s and 1990s.

Audiovisual Materials and Unpublished Personal Papers

Far and Beyond – The Story of Gershon Kaddar. Unpublished transcript of the memoirs of Gershon Kaddar (born Karl Gans), Israel, 2012. As told to Tali Bashan, edited by Michal Kaddar, translated from Hebrew by Judy Ziv and Fredi Kaddar.

Interview with Manfred Gans, conducted by Ian Dear, London, 1987. In the English language. Total running time approx. 5 hours. (In the holdings of the Imperial War Museum, London.)

Interview with Manfred Gans, conducted by Hans-Jörg Modlmayr during a visit to Borken, 1999. In the German language. Total running time approx. 5 hours. (In the holdings of the Villa ten Hompel, Münster.)

Interview with Manfred Gans, conducted by Amy Reuben, 2004. In the English language. Total running time approx. 4.5 hours. (In the holdings of the USHMM, Washington.)

Moritz Gans – Snapshots aus seinem Leben. Multi-page poem about Moritz Gans's life on the occasion of his 70th birthday, composed by his friend Ephraim Günsberg. Israel, 1955.

Remembering Ted. Unpublished memoirs of Theo Kaddar (born Theo Gans). Israel, 2018.

Unknown Warriors. A BBC Radio Wales programme about Three Troop. Running time 90 minutes. BBC, 1999.

Books

Adler, Hans G.: *Theresienstadt 1941–1945. Das Antlitz einer Zwangsgemeinschaft.* Tübingen: J. C. B. Mohr 1960.

Bauer, Christian; Rebekka Göpfert: *Die Ritchie Boys. Deutsche Emigranten beim US-Geheimdienst.* Hamburg: Hoffmann und Campe 2005.

Benz, Wolfgang: *Theresienstadt. Eine Geschichte von Täuschung und Vernichtung.* Munich. C. H. Beck 2013.

Bierhaus, August: *Es ist nicht leicht, darüber zu sprechen. Der Novemberpogrom 1938 im Kreis Borken.* Borken 1988.

Borchert, Wolfgang: 'On the Move – Generation without Farewell', in: *The Man Outside,* translated by David Porter. New York: New Directions 1971, p. 39–40. Originally published in 1947 as *Unterwegs – Generation ohne Abschied.*

Buruma, Ian: *Year Zero. A History of 1945.* London: Atlantic Books / Penguin 2013.

Dear, Ian: *Ten Commando 1942–1945*. London: Grafton Books 1989.

Fritsch, Bruno: *Engelbert Niebecker (1895–1955)*. Bielefeld: Verlag für Regionalgeschichte 2015.

Fry, Helen: *German Schoolboy, British Commando. Churchill's Secret Soldier*. Stroud: The History Press 2010.

Gans, Manfred: *Life Gave Me a Chance*. Self-published: 2010.

Glaser, Hermann: *1945 – Ein Lesebuch*. Frankfurt am Main: Fischer Taschenbuch Verlag 1995.

Hájková, Anna: *The Last Ghetto*. Oxford: Oxford University Press 2020.

Heym, Stefan: *Nachruf*. Munich: Bertelsmann 1988.

Heym, Stefan: *Schwarzenberg*. Munich: Bertelsmann 1984.

Hubalek, Claus: 'Unsre jungen Jahre', in: *Die Stunde Eins. Erzählungen, Reportagen, Essays aus der Nachkriegszeit*. Munich: Deutscher Taschenbuchverlag 1982, pp. 8–12.

Hüser, Karl: *'Unschuldig' in britischer Lagerhaft? Das Internierungslager No. 5 Staumühle 1945–1948*. Cologne: SH-Verlag 1999.

Katzenstein, Willy: 'Emigrantensong'. London 1939

Kern, Steven: *Jewish Refugees from Germany and Austria in the British Army, 1939–45*. Nottingham: University of Nottingham 2004.

Leasor, James: *Codename Nimrod*. Boston: Houghton 1980

Leighton-Langer, Peter: *X steht für unbekannt. Deutsche und Österreicher in den britischen Streitkräften im Zweiten Weltkrieg*. Berlin: Berlin Verlag 1999.

Lieb, Peter: *Unternehmen Overlord. Die Invasion in der Normandie und die Befreiung Europas*. Munich: C. H. Beck 2014.

Lustiger, Arno: *Zum Kampf auf Leben und Tod. Das Buch vom Widerstand der Juden 1933–1945*. Cologne: Kiepenheuer & Witsch 1994.

Masters, Peter: *Striking Back. A Jewish Commando's War against the Nazis.* Novato: Presidio 1997.

Müller, Helmut: *Fünf vor null. Die Besetzung des Münsterlandes 1945.* Münster: Aschendorff Verlag 2005.

Oenning, Mechtild: *Borken und die katholische Kirche zur Zeit des Nationalsozialismus.* Borken 1988.

Padover, Saul: *Experiment in Germany: The story of an American intelligence officer.* Duell, Sloan and Pearce, New York 1946.

Pracht-Jörns, Elfi: *Jüdisches Kulturerbe in Nordrhein-Westfalen. Teil IV: Regierungsbezirk Münster.* Cologne: J. P. Bachem Verlag 2002.

Schöneberg, Mechtild; Thomas Ridder; Norbert Fasse: *Die Jüdischen Gemeinden in Borken und Gemen.* Bielefeld: Verlag für Regionalgeschichte 2010.

Ullrich, Volker: *Acht Tage im Mai. Die letzten Wochen des Dritten Reichs.* Munich. C. H. Beck 2020.

Wehler, Hans-Ulrich: *Deutsche Gesellschaftsgeschichte, Band 4: Vom Beginn des Ersten Weltkrieges bis zur Gründung der beiden deutschen Staaten 1914 – 1949.* Munich. C. H. Beck 2008.

Wember, Heiner: *Umerziehung im Lager. Internierung und Bestrafung von Nationalsozialisten in der britischen Besatzungszone Deutschlands.* Essen: Klartext Verlag 2007.

Articles and Papers

Benz, Wolfgang: Zwischen Amnesie und Erinnerungskultur – Die Deutschen und der 8. Mai 1945, in: *Deutschland Archiv*, 24 May 2019, available online at: www.bpb.de/291762.

'Commando Troop was all German', in: *Daily Express*, 24 October 1946, p. 5.

Fasse, Norbert: '. . . all die Geisteskämpfe, die unbewußt die Volksseele durchkämpft': Zum 'weltanschaulichen Gepäck' des katholischen Milieus im westlichen Münsterland 1918–1933, in: *Westfälische Forschungen*, Vol. 56, 2006, pp. 237–64.

Goodman, Michael: In search of a lost Commando: a personal account of No. 3 'X' Troop, No. 10 Inter-Allied Commando, in: *Journal of Intelligence History*, Vol. 15, 2016, pp. 42–58.

Gulland, Diana: Basque and Jewish refugees at Tythrop House, Kingsey, 1937 to 1940, in: *Records of Buckinghamshire*, Vol. 54, 2014, pp. 179–200.

Hájková, Anna: 'Poor devils' of the Camps. Dutch Jews in Theresienstadt, 1943–1945, in: *Yad Vashem Studies*, Vol. 43, 2015, pp. 77–111.

Hammerstein, Katrin; Birgit Hofmann: 'Wir [. . .] müssen die Vergangenheit annehmen' – Richard von Weizsäckers Rede zum Kriegsende 1985, in: *Deutschland Archiv*, 18 December 2015, available online at: www.bpb.de/217619.

Jeffreys-Jones, Rhodri: Inter-Allied Commando Intelligence and Security Training in Gwynedd: The Coates Memoir, in: *Intelligence and National Security*, Vol. 30, 2015, pp. 545–59.

Lobeck, Lenore: Missbraucht und entzaubert – der Mythos der Freien Republik Schwarzenberg, in: *Deutschland Archiv*, 7 May 2020, available online at: www.bpb.de/308577.

Lordick, Harald: Das Landwerk Neuendorf 1932–1943 – Berufsumschichtung, Hachschara, Zwangsarbeit, in: Pilarczyk, Ulrike; Ofer Ashkenazi: Arne Homann (Eds.): *Hachschara und Jugend-Alija. Wege jüdischer Jugend nach Palästina 1918–1941.* Gifhorn 2020, pp. 135–63.

Löw, Andrea: Widerstand und Selbstbehauptung von Juden im Nationalsozialismus, in: *Aus Politik und Zeitgeschichte (APUZ)*, Vol. 27, 2014, available online at: www.bpb.de/ apuz/186872.

Vogt, Adolf: 'Werwölfe' hinter Stacheldraht – Das Interniertencamp Recklinghausen-Hillerheide (1945–1948), in: *Vestische Zeitschrift. Recklinghausen 1994–1997*, pp. 395–472.

Weizsäcker, Richard: Rede zur Gedenkveranstaltung zum 40 Jahrestag des Endes des Zweiten Weltkrieges in Europa, 8/5/1985, available online at http://www.bundespraesident.de/SharedDocs/Downloads/DE/Reden/2015/02/150202-RvW-Rede-8-Mai-1985.pdf. English version available online at bundespraesident.de/SharedDocs/Downloads/DE/Reden/2015/02/150202-RvW-Rede-8-Mai-1985-englisch.pdf?__blob=publicationFile.

Westerhoff, Hermann; Achim Wiedemann: 'Dann gaot wej no Dobbs!' Lieutenant Colonel Cyril Montague Dobbs, 1945 bis 1949 Kommandant des 208 Military Government Detachment und 'Kreis Resident Officer' in Borken, in: *Unser Bocholt. Zeitschrift für Kultur und Heimatpflege, Jahrgang 63*, 2012, pp. 5–19.

Selected Internet Resources

http://gegendasvergessen-borken.de/index.html
   This site contains several short biographies and genealogies of Borken Jews. It is the result of a school project run by the working group Jüdisches Leben in Borken und Gemen.

http://www.ghetto-theresienstadt.de/index.htm
   Privately run, comprehensive online encyclopaedia of the Theresienstadt ghetto.

https://www.jewishvirtuallibrary.org/no-3-jewish-troop-of-the-no-10-commando

Database of the members of Three Troop, No. 10 (Inter-Allied) Commando.

https://www.pamatnik-terezin.cz

Official website of the Terezín Memorial, which includes an online database with information on former inmates.

https://www.yadvashem.org

Contains the largest database of the victims of the Holocaust as well as countless collections and dossiers, including on Jewish units that fought against the Nazi regime.